# English Missions!

## Basic

Robert Hickling
Misato Usukura

**KINSEIDO**

**Kinseido Publishing Co., Ltd.**
3-21 Kanda Jimbo-cho, Chiyoda-ku,
Tokyo 101-0051, Japan

Copyright © 2019 by Robert Hickling
　　　　　　　　  Misato Usukura

*All rights reserved. No part of this publication may be reproduced, stored in a retrieval system, or transmitted, in any form or by any means, electronic, mechanical, photocopying, recording or otherwise, without the prior permission of the publisher.*

First published 2019 by Kinseido Publishing Co., Ltd.

Design　　　　Nampoosha Co., Ltd.
Illustrations　Toru Igarashi

Photos
P.18 ©Mira Agron | Dreamstime.com (c)
P.36 ©Lyubomir Zpgrafski | Dreamstime.com (1)
　　　©Biguail | Dreamstime.com (2)
　　　©Jose Gil | Dreamstime.com (3)
　　　©Littleny | Dreamstime.com (4)
P.84 ©Bumbleedee | Dreamstime.com (a)
　　　©Romrodinka | Dreamstime.com (b)
　　　©Tatiana Morozova | Dreamstime.com (c)
　　　©Giuseppemasci | Dreamstime.com (d)
P.96 ©Lifeinc23 | Dreamstime.com

## 音声ファイル無料ダウンロード

https://www.kinsei-do.co.jp/download/4071

この教科書で 🎧 DL 00 の表示がある箇所の音声は、上記 URL または QR コードにて無料でダウンロードできます。自習用音声としてご活用ください。

▶ PC からのダウンロードをお勧めします。スマートフォンなどでダウンロードされる場合は、ダウンロード前に「解凍アプリ」をインストールしてください。
▶ URL は、検索ボックスではなくアドレスバー(URL 表示欄) に入力してください。
▶ お使いのネットワーク環境によっては、ダウンロードできない場合があります。

◎ CD 00 　左記の表示がある箇所の音声は、教室用 CD（Class Audio CD）に収録されています。

# はしがき

*English Missions! Basic*は4技能をバランスよく使いながら英語の基礎を学ぶことができる教科書です。ニューヨークの旅行会社でインターンシップをすることになった大学生のマサが、インターンシップ先で出会った人たちと交流し、成長していく姿を通して、「仕事で英語を使う」ことをイメージしながら英語表現や基本的な文法事項を学びます。また、ニューヨークでの生活やアメリカ文化についての情報も盛りだくさんです。全15ユニットで、各ユニットは6ページで構成されています。各ユニットの構成は次のようになっています。

## Mission!

各ユニットには、3つのMission!が設定されています。Mission!をクリアすることを目指して学びましょう。

### Getting Ready

A Conversationの会話文に登場する重要な語彙の意味を確認します。（2〜3分）
B イラストを見ながら4つの短い英文を聞いて、T／F問題に答えます。（2〜3分）

### Conversation

A 会話を聞いて、内容に関するT／F問題に答えます。（5分）
B もう一度会話を聞いて、会話中の空所を埋めます。（5分）

### Mission! 1

会話文中から、「お礼を言う」「感想を述べる」などの会話表現を探して線を引き、その表現をもとに短いセリフを完成させる活動です。完成したセリフは声に出して繰り返し練習し、覚えるようにしましょう。日常生活やビジネスの場面でも使える会話表現が盛り込まれています。（2〜3分）

### Breaking Down the Grammar

ターゲットとなる文法項目を、豊富な例文と簡潔な日本語の説明で学びます。冒頭には「基本例文」が示されていますので、まずはこの文を覚えましょう。（10分）

### Grammar Checking

A 選択肢式の文法練習問題（8問）です。（10分）
B 文法項目への理解を確かにするための練習問題です。ここでは、文の並べ替えや書き換え、穴埋め問題など、文法項目によって問題形式に変化をつけています。（10分）

## Mission! 2

学んだ文法項目を使って、フル・センテンスの英作文に挑戦します。辞書を使ったり、ヒントとして与えられている語句を参考にしたりして、自分で英文を組み立てる力を身につけましょう。(5分)

## Reading

**A** 主人公のマサがインターンシップを通して知ったこと・経験したことなどについて綴った日誌 (Masa's Log) を読みます。写真やイラスト・図版などの視覚情報を、読んだ内容と照らし合わせて答える問題がついています。写真を時系列に並べ替えたり、内容に合うイラストを選んだりと、英文の概要を把握するのに役立つ形式となっています。(5分)

**B** 内容に関する選択肢式の問題です。より詳細な情報を確認しましょう。(5分)

## Wrap-Up Writing

**A** 短い文書を読み取ります。日常生活のタイムスケジュール、会社で使われる注文票、病院で記入する問診票など、テーマは多岐にわたります。(5分)

**B** **A**の情報を参照しながら、穴埋め形式で短いパラグラフを完成させる問題です。ターゲットとなる文法項目を正しく使えるようになっているか、確認しましょう。また、ここで完成した英文は、後に続くMission! 3でモデル文として使われます。(5分)

## Mission! 3

Wrap-Up Writingの**A** **B**で学んだことを生かし、自分自身について短いパラグラフを書く活動です。**B**のモデル文の型を意識し、Hintsとして与えられている語句も参考にしながら、自分だけのオリジナルの英文を作成してみましょう。(15分)

この他、巻末には付録として会話表現 & 基本例文一覧 (各ユニットのMission! 1で取り上げた表現とBreaking Down the Grammarの基本例文の空所補充問題) と不規則変化動詞一覧も用意しました。予習・復習にぜひご活用ください。

最後に、本書の作成にあたり、金星堂の皆様から多くのご助言、ご支援をいただいただけでなく、多大なご尽力を賜りました。この場をお借りして御礼申し上げます。

著者一同

# 本書は CheckLink（チェックリンク）対応テキストです。

 CheckLink のアイコンが表示されている設問は、CheckLink に対応しています。

CheckLink を使用しなくても従来通りの授業ができますが、特色をご理解いただき、授業活性化のためにぜひご活用ください。

## CheckLink の特色について

　大掛かりで複雑な従来の e-learning システムとは異なり、CheckLink のシステムは大きな特色として次の3点が挙げられます。
1．これまで行われてきた教科書を使った授業展開に大幅な変化を加えることなく、専門的な知識なしにデジタル学習環境を導入することができる。
2．PC 教室や CALL 教室といった最新の機器が導入された教室に限定されることなく、普通教室を使用した授業でもデジタル学習環境を導入することができる。
3．授業中での使用に特化し、教師・学習者双方のモチベーション・集中力をアップさせ、授業自体を活性化することができる。

### ▶教科書を使用した授業に「デジタル学習環境」を導入できる
　本システムでは、学習者は教科書の CheckLink のアイコンが表示されている設問に PC やスマートフォン、携帯電話端末からインターネットを通して解答します。そして教師は、授業中にリアルタイムで解答結果を把握し、正解率などに応じて有効な解説を行うことができるようになっています。教科書自体は従来と何ら変わりはありません。解答の手段として CheckLink を使用しない場合でも、従来通りの教科書として使用して授業を行うことも、もちろん可能です。

### ▶教室環境を選ばない
　従来の多機能な e-learning 教材のように学習者側の画面に多くの機能を持たせることはせず、「解答する」ことに機能を特化しました。PC だけでなく、一部タブレット端末やスマートフォン、携帯電話端末からの解答も可能です。したがって、PC 教室や CALL 教室といった大掛かりな教室は必要としません。普通教室でも CheckLink を用いた授業が可能です。教師は PC だけでなく、一部タブレット端末やスマートフォンからも解答結果の確認をすることができます。

### ▶授業を活性化するための支援システム
　本システムは予習や復習のツールとしてではなく、授業中に活用されることで真価を発揮する仕組みになっています。CheckLink というデジタル学習環境を通じ、教師と学習者双方が授業中に解答状況などの様々な情報を共有することで、学習者はやる気を持って解答し、教師は解答状況に応じて効果的な解説を行う、という好循環を生み出します。CheckLink は、普段の授業をより活力のあるものへと変えていきます。

　上記3つの大きな特色以外にも、掲示板などの授業中に活用できる機能を用意しています。従来通りの教科書としても使用はできますが、ぜひ CheckLink の機能をご理解いただき、普段の授業をより活性化されたものにしていくためにご活用ください。

# CheckLink の使い方

CheckLinkは、PCや一部タブレット端末、スマートフォン、携帯電話端末を用いて、この教科書の ⏴CheckLink のアイコン表示のある設問に解答するシステムです。
- 初めてCheckLinkを使う場合、以下の要領で**「学習者登録」**と**「教科書登録」**を行います。
- 一度登録を済ませれば、あとは毎回**「ログイン画面」**から入るだけです。CheckLinkを使う教科書が増えたときだけ、改めて**「教科書登録」**を行ってください。

## CheckLink URL

https://checklink.kinsei-do.co.jp/student/

QRコードの読み取りができる端末の場合はこちらから ▶▶▶

**ご注意ください!** 上記URLは**「検索ボックス」**でなく**「アドレスバー(URL表示欄)」**に入力してください。

### ▶学習者登録

① 上記URLにアクセスすると、右のページが表示されます。学校名を入力し「ログイン画面へ」をクリックしてください。
**PCの場合は「PC用はこちら」**をクリックしてPC用ページを表示します。同様に学校名を入力し「ログイン画面へ」をクリックしてください。

② ログイン画面が表示されたら**「初めての方はこちら」**をクリックし「学習者登録画面」に入ります。

③ 自分の学籍番号、氏名、メールアドレス(学校のメールなど**PCメールを推奨**)を入力し、次に**任意のパスワード**を8桁以上20桁未満(半角英数字)で入力します。なお、学籍番号はパスワードとして使用することはできません。

④ 「パスワード確認」は、❸で入力したパスワードと同じものを入力します。

⑤ 最後に「登録」ボタンをクリックして登録は完了です。次回からは、「ログイン画面」から学籍番号とパスワードを入力してログインしてください。

## ▶教科書登録

①ログイン後、メニュー画面から「教科書登録」を選び（PCの場合はその後「新規登録」ボタンをクリック）、「教科書登録」画面を開きます。

②教科書と受講する授業を登録します。
教科書の最終ページにある、**教科書固有番号**のシールをはがし、印字された**16桁の数字とアルファベット**を入力します。

③授業を担当される先生から連絡された**11桁の授業ID**を入力します。

④最後に「登録」ボタンをクリックして登録は完了です。

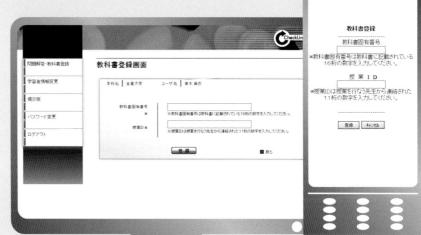

⑤実際に使用する際は「教科書一覧」（PCの場合は「教科書選択画面」）の該当する教科書名をクリックすると、「問題解答」の画面が表示されます。

## ▶問題解答

①問題は教科書を見ながら解答します。この教科書の CheckLink のアイコン表示のある設問に解答できます。

②問題が表示されたら選択肢を選びます。

③表示されている問題に解答した後、「解答」ボタンをクリックすると解答が登録されます。

## ▶CheckLink 推奨環境

**PC**

推奨 OS
　Windows 7, 10 以降
　MacOS X 以降

推奨ブラウザ
　Internet Explorer 8.0 以上
　Firefox 40.0 以上
　Google Chrome 50 以上
　Safari

**携帯電話・スマートフォン**
　3G 以降の携帯電話（docomo, au, softbank）
　iPhone, iPad（iOS9 〜）
　Android OS スマートフォン、タブレット

・最新の推奨環境についてはウェブサイトをご確認ください。
・上記の推奨環境を満たしている場合でも、機種によってはご利用いただけない場合もあります。また、推奨環境は技術動向等により変更される場合があります。

## ▶CheckLink 開発

CheckLink は奥田裕司 福岡大学教授、正興 IT ソリューション株式会社、株式会社金星堂によって共同開発されました。

CheckLink は株式会社金星堂の登録商標です。

---

**CheckLink の使い方に関するお問い合わせは…**

正興ITソリューション株式会社　CheckLink 係

**e-mail**　checklink@seiko-denki.co.jp

# English Missions! Basic

## Table of Contents

People & Places —————————————————— 10

Pre-unit [基本語順] —————————————————— 12

**Unit 1** Welcome to the "Big Apple" 現在形 —————— 14

**Unit 2** What's the Boss Like? 代名詞 —————————— 20

**Unit 3** Masa's First Day on the Job 前置詞 —————— 26

**Unit 4** Summer Fun 過去形 ————————————————— 32

**Unit 5** Hotel Guest Satisfaction 可算名詞・不可算名詞 — 38

**Unit 6** Brainstorming 進行形 ———————————————— 44

**Unit 7** Glad to Be of Service WH疑問文 ——————— 50

**Unit 8** Socializing with Co-Workers 動名詞・不定詞 —— 56

**Unit 9** Vacation Spots 未来形 ——————————————— 62

**Unit 10** Sports Talk 比較級・最上級 ——————————— 68

**Unit 11** Tour Day 助動詞 ————————————————— 74

**Unit 12** Party Time! 現在完了形 ————————————— 80

**Unit 13** Office Meeting 関係詞 —————————————— 86

**Unit 14** A Bit of History 受動態 ————————————— 92

**Unit 15** Farewell, Masa and Lucy 接続詞 ——————— 98

会話表現 & 基本例文一覧 ————————————————— 104

不規則変化動詞一覧 ————————————————————— 107

# People & Places

この教科書に登場する人や場所を紹介します。

**ナカタ・マサヒロ**
愛称「マサ」
日本の大学に通う21歳

夏休みを利用して、アメリカのニューヨークにある旅行代理店・プリーズトラベル社でインターンシップに挑戦する。
趣味は一人旅と野球。将来は旅行会社や航空会社など、旅行に関わる仕事に就くことを夢みている。

## ニューヨーク市について

アメリカ東部、ニューヨーク州の東南部、ハドソン川河口の港湾に位置するアメリカ最大の都市です。Bronx（ブロンクス）、Brooklyn（ブルックリン）、Manhattan（マンハッタン）、Queens（クイーンズ）、Staten Island（スタテンアイランド）の5つの行政区（Borough）に分かれています。

ヒップホップやグラフィティー発祥の地。ニューヨークヤンキースのホームグラウンド「ヤンキースタジアム」があるのもここブロンクスです。

ニューヨークの中心街。山手線内と同じくらいの広さです。タイムズスクエア、セントラルパーク、ウォール街、ブロードウェイ、MoMAなど有名観光名所の多くがここマンハッタンにあります。

スタテンアイランドはニューヨーク湾の入り口に位置します。わずかながらニューヨーク開拓当時の面影を残し、住宅地ののどかな風景が広がります。

ブルックリンは住宅街として発展し、文化の発信地でもあります。おしゃれな飲食店やカフェ、古着屋なども多く、街歩きを楽しめるスポットとしても有名です。

アメリカの中でももっとも多民族が居住すると言われている地区。ニューヨークと世界各国を結ぶJFK空港とラガーディア空港はともにクイーンズにあります。

# プリーズトラベル社で働く人々

**Please Travel Company** (プリーズトラベル社) って?
ニューヨーク・マンハッタンにある旅行代理店。ニューヨーク市近郊の観光案内ツアーから海外リゾートまで、幅広く手がける。アットホームな社風で、国際色豊かな社員が在籍。マサはここで様々な人と出会い、インターンシップを通じて成長していきます。

## Patricia Anderson
愛称 Patty (パティ)

大学卒業後、プリーズトラベル社に入社。ツアーコンダクターからパッケージツアーの企画まで幅広くこなし、同僚からの信頼も厚い。
サービス精神が旺盛で努力家。

## Theodore Brown
愛称 Ted (テッド)

プリーズトラベル社のマネージャー。大らかな性格で、部下とも気さくに、分け隔てなく接する。
ニューヨーク・ヤンキースとビールをこよなく愛す。

## Lucy Tan
愛称 Lucy (ルーシー)

シンガポール出身の大学生。マサと同時期にプリーズトラベル社のインターンシップに参加。
趣味はパン作りとアクセサリー集め。将来の夢はシンガポールでニューヨーク・スタイルのカフェを開くこと。

# Pre-unit

このユニットでは英語の基本語順を勉強します。日本語では「私たちは英語を勉強します」のように「〜は」「〜を」といった助詞を使いますが、英語には助詞がなくWe study English.のように語句を並べて文を作ります。語順が変わると意味も変わります。

● **英語の基本語順**：英語では主語の次に動詞が来ます。

（例）

| 誰が(主語) | どうする(動詞) | 何を | 意味 |
|---|---|---|---|
| I | have | three cats. | 私は猫を３匹飼っています。 |
| John | plays | the guitar. | ジョンはギターを弾きます。 |

## Check! ✓

**A** 語順に注意して、次の２つの英文の意味を書きましょう。

**1.** Takashi loves Maiko.

_____

**2.** Maiko hates tomatoes.　　　　　　　　　　　　　　　　　　hate「〜を嫌う」

_____

**B** (　　) 内の語句を並べ替えて英文を作りましょう。

**1.** 私は野球をします。( baseball / I / play )

_____

**2.** 私たちは経済学を学びます。( economics / study / we )

_____

● 基本語順＋追加情報

基本語順　　　　　　　　　　　　追加情報

（例）

| 誰が(主語) | どうする(動詞) | 何を | 追加情報 | 意味 |
|---|---|---|---|---|
| John | plays | the guitar | every day. | ジョンは毎日ギターを弾きます。 |
| Kei and I | take care of | the rabbit | at school. | ケイと私は学校でウサギを世話します。 |

## Check! ✓

Ⓐ 語順に注意して、次の２つの英文の意味を書きましょう。

1. Akiko makes apple pies with her sister.

2. We have breakfast at a café on Sundays.

Ⓑ (　　) 内の語句を並べ替えて英文を作りましょう。

1. 私は毎日犬を散歩させます。( my dog / every day / I / walk )

2. 私の母は庭でトマトを育てています。( in the garden / tomatoes / my mother / grows )

3. 私たちは毎週木曜日に体育館で剣道の練習をします。
　　　　　　　　( kendo / in the gym / practice / we / every Thursday )

# Unit 1

# Welcome to the "Big Apple"

**Mission**
- お礼を伝える
- 動詞の現在形を理解する
- 自己紹介をする

## Getting Ready

**A** 英語の意味に合う日本語をa〜eから選びましょう。

CheckLink　DL 02　CD 02

1. Welcome to the "Big Apple."　(　)　　a. 時差ボケ
2. business card　　　　　　　　 (　)　　b. ビッグアップルにようこそ
3. My pleasure.　　　　　　　　　(　)　　c. フライト、飛行便
4. flight　　　　　　　　　　　　(　)　　d. 名刺
5. jet lag　　　　　　　　　　　　(　)　　e. どういたしまして

**B** 空港にいるマサ(Masa)とパティ(Patty)のイラストを見ながら1〜4の英文を聞きましょう。イラストと合っていればT、異なっていればFを選びましょう。

CheckLink　DL 03　CD 03

1. T / F　　2. T / F　　3. T / F　　4. T / F

## Conversation
### Does Masa Have Jet Leg or Jet Lag?

ニューヨークのJFK空港に到着したマサを、パティが出迎えてくれています。

**A** 会話を聞きましょう。1～4について、聞き取った内容と合っていればT、異なっていればFを選びましょう。

CheckLink　DL 04　CD 04

1. New York's nickname is the "Big Apple."　( T / F )
2. Patricia asks Masa to call her Tricia.　( T / F )
3. Masa doesn't have jet lag.　( T / F )
4. It's early in the morning in Tokyo now.　( T / F )

**B** もう一度会話を聞いて、空所を埋めましょう。その後ペアになって、会話の練習をしましょう。

**Masa:** Excuse me, I'm Masahiro Nakata. ($^1$　　　) you Patricia?
**Patty:** Masahiro! Yes, ($^2$　　　) Patricia. Welcome to the "Big Apple."
**Masa:** The big apple? I ($^3$　　　) understand.
**Patty:** It's a nickname for New York. Here, let me give you my business card. It ($^4$　　　) Patricia, but please call me Patty.
**Masa:** And everyone ($^5$　　　) me Masa. Thanks for meeting me at the airport.
**Patty:** My pleasure. It's a long flight from Tokyo. Do you ($^6$　　　) jet lag?
**Masa:** Jet leg? *(pointing at his leg)*
**Patty:** Ha ha ha! Not l-e-g, l-a-g. I ($^7$　　　), are you tired from your long flight?
**Masa:** Oh! Yes, I'm quite tired. ($^8$　　　) 5:00 a.m. in Tokyo now.

### Mission ! 1. お礼の表現を使ってみよう！

マサがパティにお礼を言っている英文を探し、線を引きましょう。また、それを真似て次のセリフを言ってみましょう。

_____ for _____ to New York.
ニューヨークに来てくれてありがとう。

## Breaking Down the Grammar  ● 現在形

**基本例文** I **am** from Japan.  I **work** in New York.
私は日本出身です。ニューヨークで働いています。

■ be 動詞は主語の状態や性質を表すときに使います。主語に合わせて形が変わります。

| 組み合わせ<br>「主語(誰が) ＋ be 動詞」 | | 主語を説明することば<br>「どうだ」 | 意味 |
|---|---|---|---|
| I | am | a university student. | 私は大学生です。 |
| You | are | kind. | あなたは親切です。 |
| He / She / It | is | wonderful. | 彼/彼女/それはすばらしいです。 |
| We / You / They | are | good friends. | 私たち/あなた(たち)/彼らはよい友人です。 |

[否定文] I **am** [**I'm**] **not** a university student.  私は大学生ではありません。
[疑問文] **Is Mary** good at singing?  メアリーは歌が得意ですか。

■ be 動詞以外の動詞を一般動詞と呼び、主語の動作・状態・性質を表すときに使います。

| 主語 | 一般動詞 | その他の情報 | 意味 |
|---|---|---|---|
| I | live | in New York. | 私はニューヨークに住んでいます。 |
| John | likes | rock music. | ジョンはロック音楽が好きです。 |
| Lisa and I | play | soccer every Sunday. | リサと私は毎週日曜日にサッカーをします。 |

▶ 主語が I / You 以外の単数形で時制が現在の場合、一般動詞の語尾に -s[-es] をつけます。

[否定文]
I **don't live** in New York.
私はニューヨークに住んでいません。

[疑問文]
**Does John like** rock music?
ジョンはロック音楽が好きですか。

My dad is a dentist. He hurts people all day.

# Grammar Checking

**A** (　) 内から正しい選択肢を選び、文を完成させましょう。

1. Patty ( **a.** live   **b.** does live   **c.** lives ) in New York.
2. ( **a.** Are   **b.** Do   **c.** Does ) Mr. and Mrs. Jackson have any children?
3. This building ( **a.** aren't   **b.** isn't   **c.** doesn't ) very old.
4. Saki ( **a.** is   **b.** does   **c.** isn't ) never late for class.
5. Please ( **a.** calling   **b.** to call   **c.** call ) me tonight.
6. ( **a.** Are   **b.** Does   **c.** Is ) Joe married?
7. Linda and her sister ( **a.** has   **b.** have   **c.** are having ) a dog.
8. He ( **a.** doesn't have   **b.** isn't having   **c.** doesn't has ) his textbook today.

**B** (　) 内の語句を並べ替えて、日本語に合う文を作りましょう。

1. ( intern / Masa / an / is )　マサはインターンです。

   _____.

2. ( afraid / bugs / you / of / are )　あなたは虫を怖がっているのですか。

   _____?

3. ( very / Luke / doesn't / TV / watch / often )　ルークはあまりテレビを見ません。

   _____.

4. ( train / station / stop / does / at / this / every )　この電車は各駅停車ですか。

   _____?

## Mission ! 2. 動詞の現在形を使ってみよう！

次の日本語を英語に直しましょう。

1. パトリシア（Patricia）は旅行会社に勤めています。　　　＊〜に勤める  work for

   _____

2. あなたは毎朝早く起きますか。

   _____

# Reading  *Masa's Log*

**A** マサのインターン日記を読み、写真a〜dを紹介されている順に並べ替えましょう。

## The Big Apple

I'm in New York City, the Big Apple. There are so many things to do and see here. Manhattan is an island in New York with many tall buildings. I love Times Square! It's a famous entertainment area in Manhattan. Many people go there. It's really exciting! Central Park is a huge park in the middle of Manhattan. Forty million people visit it each year. New York is also famous for the Statue of Liberty. It's on Liberty Island.

¹(     ) ➡ ²(     ) ➡ ³(     ) ➡ ⁴(     )

**B** 英文をもう一度読み、正しい選択肢を選びましょう。

1. Manhattan is ( **a.** an area of New York    **b.** a tall building in New York ).
2. Times Square is ( **a.** a business district    **b.** an entertainment district ).
3. The Statue of Liberty is ( **a.** in Central Park    **b.** on Liberty Island ).

# Wrap-Up Writing

**A** これはマサのプロフィールです。情報を読み取りましょう。

Name: Masahiro Nakata
Place of birth: Tokyo
Birthday: August 30    Age: 21
Personality: cheerful, energetic
Interests ☺: traveling, English
Dislikes ☹: spicy food, shopping

*Notes:* personality「性格」 energetic「活動的な」 interests「趣味」

**B** A の情報を文にまとめてみましょう。

His name is _____ Nakata. He is from _____.

His _____ is August 30. He is _____ years old. He is cheerful

and _____. His interests _____ traveling and _____.

He doesn't like spicy food or shopping.

## Mission ! 3. あなた自身について書いてみよう！

A と B を参考にして、自己紹介文を書いてみましょう。

My name is _____

_____

_____

_____

**Hints**
quiet「静かな」 shy「恥ずかしがりやの」 outgoing「社交的な」 talkative「話し好きな」
drawing pictures「絵を描くこと」 surfing the net「ネットサーフィンをすること」
vegetables「野菜」 homework「宿題」

# Unit 2 What's the Boss Like?

**Mission**
- 感想を述べる
- 代名詞の使い方に慣れる
- 友人を紹介する

## Getting Ready

**A** 英語の意味に合う日本語をa〜eから選びましょう。

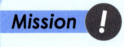 CheckLink　DL 06　CD 06

1. actually　　　　（　）　　a. 楽しみにする
2. popular　　　　（　）　　b. 心の広い
3. look forward to（　）　　c. 実は
4. open-minded　　（　）　　d. 意見
5. opinion　　　　（　）　　e. 人気のある

**B** ベーグルカフェに集うマサたちのイラストを見ながら1〜4の英文を聞きましょう。マサに関する英文にはM、パティに関する英文にはP、ルーシーに関する英文にはL、ウェイターに関する英文にはWを書き入れましょう。

 CheckLink　DL 07　CD 07

1. (　)　　2. (　)　　3. (　)　　4. (　)

## Conversation
### An Honest Thought from Masa

パティは今日から受け入れる2人のインターン学生・マサとルーシーを朝食に招待しました。

**A** 会話を聞きましょう。1〜4について、聞き取った内容と合っていればT、異なっていればFを選びましょう。

1. Lucy never has time to make bagels. ( T / F )
2. Not many people in New York eat bagels. ( T / F )
3. Ted is Patty's boss. ( T / F )
4. Ted likes people to tell him their ideas. ( T / F )

**B** もう一度会話を聞いて、空所を埋めましょう。その後ペアになって、会話の練習をしましょう。

**Patty:** Thanks for coming this morning. (¹    ) hope you like bagels.
**Lucy:** I love (²    )! I sometimes make bagels (³    ) in Singapore.
**Masa:** Actually, this is (⁴    ) first time to try one.
**Patty:** Well, bagels are very popular in New York. …Anyway, I just want to welcome you to Please Travel. (⁵    ) look forward to working with you. Do you have any questions?
**Lucy:** Is (⁶    ) boss nice?
**Patty:** Ted? Yes, everyone likes (⁷    ). He's very friendly and open-minded. He gives his opinions, and he likes everyone to give (⁸    ). …Masa, is your bagel OK?
**Masa:** To be honest, I don't really like it.

### Mission 1. 感想を述べてみよう！

マサが食べたものの感想を言っている英文を探し、線を引きましょう。また、それを真似て次のセリフを言ってみましょう。

To _____ _____, I don't really _____ Thai food.
正直なところ、タイ料理はあまり好きではありません。

## Breaking Down the Grammar ● 代名詞

**基本例文** These cookies look delicious. I want to try **them**.
これらのクッキーはおいしそうです。私はこれらを食べてみたいです。

■ 代名詞は前に出てきた名詞を言い換えるときに使います。

Lisa is my boss.  **She** is very kind.  リサは私の上司です。彼女はとても親切です。

Sam and Jack are very tall.  **They** play on the volleyball team.
サムとジャックはとても背が高いです。彼らはバレーボール部でプレーしています。

**We** live in the Internet age.  私たちはインターネットの時代に生きています。

▶ We や They は前に指すものがなくても、「一般の人々」という意味で用いられることがあります。

■ 代名詞は、文中での働きによって形を変えます。

| 主格「～は／～が」主語になる | 所有格「～の」後ろに名詞が来る | 目的格「～を」目的語になる前置詞の後に来る | 所有代名詞「～のもの」 | 再帰代名詞「～自身」 |
|---|---|---|---|---|
| I | my | me | mine | myself |
| you | your | you | yours | yourself / yourselves |
| he | his | him | his | himself |
| she | her | her | hers | herself |
| it | its | it | — | itself |
| we | our | us | ours | ourselves |
| they | their | them | theirs | themselves |

■ 所有格の代名詞は後ろに名詞を伴いますが、所有代名詞は単体で使います。

Please tell me **your** email address.  I will tell you **mine**.
あなたのメールアドレスを教えてください。
私のもあなたにお伝えします。

■ 主語と目的語が同一人物のときは再帰代名詞を使います。

We all enjoyed **ourselves** at the party.
私たちは皆パーティーで楽しみました。

I take him for a walk every day.

# Grammar Checking

**A** ( ) 内から正しい選択肢を選び、文を完成させましょう。

1. My brother and ( **a.** I   **b.** me   **c.** mine ) are on a soccer team.
2. We talk about ( **a.** us   **b.** our   **c.** we ) work at a meeting every Friday.
3. Please give this pen to Alice. I think it's ( **a.** she   **b.** her   **c.** hers ).
4. Cathy watches movies in ( **a.** she   **b.** her   **c.** hers ) free time.
5. Excuse me, miss. Is this umbrella ( **a.** its   **b.** hers   **c.** yours )?
6. Please take off your shoes and put ( **a.** they   **b.** them   **c.** their ) here.
7. Peter always enjoys ( **a.** himself   **b.** herself   **c.** themselves ) at parties.
8. Our English teacher tells ( **a.** our   **b.** us   **c.** ourselves ) interesting stories.

**B** 空所に代名詞を入れて、対話を完成させましょう。

1. **A:** Are you and Grace American?
   **B:** Yes, _____ are from New York.
2. **A:** Do you have the time?
   **B:** Yes, _____ is 10:00.
3. **A:** These candies are delicious!
   **B:** Hmm… I don't really like _____.
4. **A:** Is this your bag, Jane?
   **B:** No, the brown one is _____.
5. **A:** Does Jim live alone?
   **B:** No, he lives with _____ grandmother.
6. **A:** Is the plate hot?
   **B:** Yes. Be careful. Don't burn _____.

## Mission  2. 代名詞を使って書いてみよう！

次の日本語を英語に直しましょう。

1. ジムは自分で髪の毛を切ります。　　　　　　　　　　　　　　＊自分で himself

   _____

2. それは私のスーツケースではありません。私のは黒です。

   _____

# Reading

● *Masa's Log*

**A** マサのインターン日記を読み、その内容に合わせて、2つのイラスト内の1〜4の空所に入る名前を選択肢から選びましょう。　CheckLink　DL 09　CD 09

## What to Call People

At the Please Travel office, we call everyone by their first name or nickname. For example, Patricia calls me Masa, and I call her Patty. Our office manager's name is Theodore Brown, but he likes everyone to call him Ted. For business, Patty's advice to me was to call someone by their last name at first, like Ms. Anderson or Mr. Brown. If Ms. Anderson later says, "Please call me Patty," or Mr. Brown says, "Everyone calls me Ted," then use that name.

● *At Please Travel…*

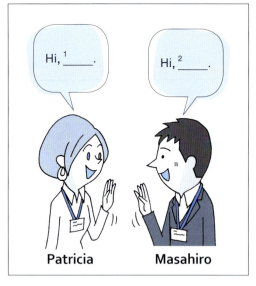

Hi, 1 ____.　Hi, 2 ____.

Patricia　Masahiro

● *Meeting a Businessperson*

Nice to meet you, 3 ____.　Nice to meet you, too. Please call me 4 ____.

Michael Jones

**a.** Masa　**b.** Mike　**c.** Mr. Jones　**d.** Patty

**B** 英文をもう一度読み、正しい選択肢を選びましょう。　CheckLink

1. At Please Travel, Masa calls Patricia ( **a.** Ms. Anderson　**b.** Patty ).
2. The office manager likes people to call him by his ( **a.** last name　**b.** nickname ).
3. For business, Patty's advice for meeting people for the first time is to call him/her Ms. or Mr. + ( **a.** first name　**b.** last name ).

# Wrap-Up Writing

**A** マサの親友シュンのプロフィールを読んでみましょう。

| | |
|---:|:---|
| **Best friend's name:** | Shunsuke Kobayashi |
| **Nickname:** | Shun |
| **How often they meet:** | about once a month |
| **Personality:** | shy, honest |
| **First met:** | junior high school |
| **Shared interest:** | watching baseball |

**Notes:** how often「どのくらいの頻度で」 first met「初対面」 shared「共通の」

**B** **A** の情報を文にまとめてみましょう。(　)には代名詞を入れてください。

Masa's best friend's name is Shunsuke ＿＿＿＿. (　) nickname is Shun.

Masa meets (　) about once a ＿＿＿＿. Shun is shy and ＿＿＿＿.

Masa first met (　) in ＿＿＿＿ high school. (　) both like

watching ＿＿＿＿.

## Mission ! 3. あなた自身について書いてみよう！

**A** と **B** を参考にして、あなたの親友について書いてみましょう。

My best friend's name is ＿＿＿＿＿＿＿＿＿＿＿＿＿＿＿＿＿＿＿＿

＿＿＿＿＿＿＿＿＿＿＿＿＿＿＿＿＿＿＿＿＿＿＿＿＿＿＿＿＿＿＿＿

＿＿＿＿＿＿＿＿＿＿＿＿＿＿＿＿＿＿＿＿＿＿＿＿＿＿＿＿＿＿＿＿

＿＿＿＿＿＿＿＿＿＿＿＿＿＿＿＿＿＿＿＿＿＿＿＿＿＿＿＿＿＿＿＿

**Hints** two or three times a month「1か月に2、3回」 friendly「親しみやすい」 hard-working「勤勉な」
elementary school「小学校」 high school「高校」 playing video games「ビデオゲームをすること」 watching movies「映画を見ること」 going to museums「美術館に行くこと」

# Unit 3 Masa's First Day on the Job

**Mission !**
- 勤務時間についてたずねる
- 前置詞の使い方に慣れる
- 行動予定について書く

## Getting Ready

**A** 英語の意味に合う日本語を a〜e から選びましょう。

CheckLink　DL 10　CD 10

1. customer　　　　（　）　　a. 勤務時間
2. work station　　（　）　　b. お客さん
3. travel agent　　 （　）　　c. 作業スペース
4. office supplies　（　）　　d. 旅行代理業者
5. office hours　　 （　）　　e. 事務用品

**B** プリーズトラベル社のカウンターのイラストを見ながら1〜4の英文を聞きましょう。イラストと合っていればT、異なっていればFを選びましょう。

CheckLink　DL 11　CD 11

1. T / F　　2. T / F　　3. T / F　　4. T / F

## Conversation ● This Is the Office

いよいよインターン開始。マサが上司のテッドにオフィスを案内してもらっています。

**A** 会話を聞きましょう。1～4について、聞き取った内容と合っていればT、異なっていればFを選びましょう。

1. Masa and Lucy have their own desks. ( T / F )
2. Masa's and Lucy's work space is in a different room. ( T / F )
3. Ted tells Masa to arrive before 10:30. ( T / F )
4. Masa is happy about his working hours. ( T / F )

**B** もう一度会話を聞いて、空所を埋めましょう。その後ペアになって、会話の練習をしましょう。

**Ted:** This is the office. The customers sit (¹       ) the counter. Work stations for our travel agents are (²       ) the counter. The copy machine, printer and office supplies are (³       ) that wall.

**Masa:** Do Lucy and I have a place to work?

**Ted:** Yes, the table and computers (⁴       ) that large window are for you.

**Masa:** Are office hours from 9:00 to 5:00?

**Ted:** No. Please arrive (⁵       ) 10:30 and 11:00 (⁶       ) the morning. Quitting time is (⁷       ) 6:30 or 7:00 p.m. We're open every day, but you and Lucy don't need to come (⁸       ) Saturdays or Sundays. Is that OK for you?

**Masa:** YES!!! I mean, yes, that's fine.

### Mission ! 1. 時間についてたずねてみよう！

マサが勤務時間についてたずねている英文を探し、線を引きましょう。また、それを真似て次のセリフを言ってみましょう。

Are office _____ _____ 8:30 _____ 4:30?

勤務時間は 8：30 から 4：30 までですか。

## Breaking Down the Grammar

  前置詞

 I often watch videos **at** home **in** the evening.
私はよく夜に家で動画を見ます。

■ 前置詞は後ろに名詞を伴って、時や場所を表します。以下は時を表す前置詞です。

| 前置詞 | 例文 |
| --- | --- |
| **at**<br>［時刻］に | The train arrives **at** 2 o'clock.<br>その電車は2時に到着します。 |
| **during**<br>［月・季節・午前／午後など］の間に | Beavers sleep **during** the daytime.<br>ビーバーは昼間は寝ています。 |
| **in**<br>［月・季節・年・午前／午後など］に | I often go for a walk **in** the afternoon.<br>私はよく午後に散歩に行きます。 |
| **on**<br>［日付や曜日］に | The exams start **on** July 10.<br>試験は7月10日に始まります。 |

■ その他の時を表す前置詞

finish work **by** 8:00「8時までに仕事を終える」 keep singing **for** two hours「2時間歌い続ける」

■ 場所を表す前置詞には以下のようなものがあります。

| 前置詞 | 例文 |
| --- | --- |
| **on**<br>〜の上に・〜に接触して | There is a large painting **on** the wall.<br>壁に大きな絵がかかっています。 |
| **near**<br>〜の近くに・で | There are two convenience stores **near** our house.<br>私たちの家の近くにはコンビニが2軒あります。 |

■ その他の場所を表す前置詞

**above** the clouds「雲の上に」　**by** the window「窓のそばに」　**over** the river「川の上に」
**next to** the building「建物の隣に」　**beside** the bank「銀行の隣に」
**between** John and Alice「ジョンとアリスの間に」
**behind** the counter「カウンターの後ろに」
**along** the street「通りに沿って」

Put them in your mouth, not in your nose.

# Grammar Checking

**A** (　) 内から正しい選択肢を選び、文を完成させましょう。

1. Misa's birthday party is ( **a.** at　**b.** in　**c.** on ) Saturday night.  Please come.
2. It's OK to drink water ( **a.** at　**b.** during　**c.** for ) class.
3. Brenda studies ( **a.** until　**b.** by　**c.** for ) three hours every night.
4. Please finish your report ( **a.** by　**b.** during　**c.** until ) Friday.
5. Look at the lovely cherry blossoms ( **a.** in　**b.** on　**c.** to ) that tree.
6. They live in a nice house ( **a.** by　**b.** above　**c.** under ) a river.
7. Airplanes fly ( **a.** above　**b.** between　**c.** below ) my house every day.
8. There's a French restaurant ( **a.** next　**b.** beside　**c.** near ) to the museum.

**B** 例にならって、空所に適当な前置詞を選択肢から選び、書き入れましょう。

| ~~at~~ | at | between | during | in | on | over |

1. My first class starts ___at___ 9:00.
2. Do you have classes _____ Saturdays?
3. Mike's birthday is _____ November.
4. Please don't talk _____ the test.
5. Andrew isn't _____ school today.  He's sick.
6. The Brooklyn Bridge goes _____ the East River.
7. In this picture, Ben is in the middle, _____ Tim and Jennifer.

## Mission　2. 前置詞を使って書いてみよう！

次の日本語を英語に直しましょう。

1. リンダ (Linda) は土曜日、10時から6時まで働いています。

2. 私の大学の近くに小さな公園があります。

# Reading

*Masa's Log*

**A** マサのインターン日記を読み、1〜4の各項目について内容と一致するほうのイラストを選びましょう。

CheckLink　DL 13　CD 13

### Please Travel: Day 1

Today was my first day of work. It takes about 45 minutes from my share house in Brooklyn to the Please Travel office in Manhattan. From home, it takes five minutes to walk to the subway station. After getting off the train, it's another five-minute walk to the office. My day at Please Travel was very busy. After work, there was a welcome party for Lucy and me at an Italian restaurant beside the office. We were the last customers to leave. It was midnight!

**1.** プリーズトラベル社の所在地

**2.** マサの交通手段

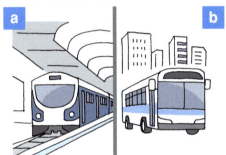

**3.** 職場での様子

**4.** パーティーで食べたもの

**B** 英文をもう一度読み、正しい選択肢を選びましょう。　CheckLink

1. To get to work, Masa rides the subway for about ( **a.** 35　**b.** 45 ) minutes.
2. There's a station ( **a.** near　**b.** far from ) Masa's share house.
3. Masa was at the restaurant until ( **a.** 10:00 p.m.　**b.** 12:00 a.m. )

# Wrap-Up Writing

**A** 普段は日本の大学に通っているマサの月曜日の予定を読んでみましょう。

**Monday Schedule**
- MORNING: classes × 2 (8:50 - 12:20)
- LUNCH: cafeteria (12:20 - 1:20)
- AFTERNOON: classes × 2 (1:20 - 4:50)
- NIGHT: home – study (1 hour), watch TV (2 hours)

**B** **A** の情報を文にまとめてみましょう。(　　) には前置詞を入れてください。

Masa has two classes (　　) Monday morning, (　　) 8:50 to 12:20. After his second class, he has lunch (　　) the cafeteria. He has two more classes (　　) the _____, starting at 1:20. His last class finishes (　　) 4:50. (　　) night, he usually stays home. He studies (　　) one hour and watches TV (　　) two hours.

## Mission  3. あなた自身について書いてみよう！

**A** と **B** を参考にして、あなたの一般的な平日のスケジュールについて書いてみましょう。

I have _____ classes _____

_____

_____

_____

**Hints**
on the campus lawn「大学の芝生で」　at a hamburger shop「ハンバーガー屋で」
work part-time「アルバイトをする」　cook dinner「夕飯を作る」　listen to music「音楽を聞く」
post photos on Instagram「インスタグラムに写真を投稿する」

# Unit 4 Summer Fun

**Mission**
- 週末にしたことを述べる
- 動詞の過去形を理解する
- ある1日を振り返る

## Getting Ready

**A** 英語の意味に合う日本語をa～eから選びましょう。

1. boardwalk ( )
2. amusement park ( )
3. roller coaster ( )
4. view ( )
5. scared ( )

a. 怖がっている
b. 眺め
c. 遊園地
d. 遊歩道
e. ジェットコースター

**B** マサとルーシーが先週末に訪れたビーチのイラストを見ながら1～4の英文を聞きましょう。イラストと合っていればT、異なっていればFを選びましょう。

1. T / F　　2. T / F　　3. T / F　　4. T / F

## Conversation ● A Day at Coney Island

マサがパティに、先週末コニー・アイランドに訪れたことを話しています。

**A** 会話を聞きましょう。1〜4について、聞き取った内容と合っていればT、異なっていればFを選びましょう。

1. Saturday was a very hot day. ( T / F )
2. Lucy and Masa went swimming at the beach. ( T / F )
3. It was Lucy's idea to ride the roller coaster. ( T / F )
4. Lucy enjoyed the view from the top of the roller coaster. ( T / F )

**B** もう一度会話を聞いて、空所を埋めましょう。その後ペアになって、会話の練習をしましょう。

**Patty:** Hi Masa. Did you (¹           ) a nice weekend?
**Masa:** Yes, Lucy and I went to Coney Island on Saturday. The weather was good. It (²           ) too hot.
**Patty:** I love Coney Island! Did you (³           ) along the boardwalk?
**Masa:** Yes, and the beach. We also (⁴           ) to one of the amusement parks there. Lucy (⁵           ) to ride the Cyclone.
**Patty:** The Cyclone. That's my favorite roller coaster! Did you like the view from the top?
**Masa:** Umm… well… actually, I (⁶           ) see anything. I was so scared, I (⁷           ) my eyes closed the whole time. …But Lucy (⁸           ) it was good.
**Patty:** Oh! Ha ha ha!

### Mission ! 1. 週末にしたことを話してみよう！

マサが土曜にルーシーと行った場所を述べている英文を探し、線を引きましょう。また、それを真似て次のセリフを言ってみましょう。

I _____ _____ the fireworks festival _____ Sunday.
私は日曜に花火大会に行きました。

## Breaking Down the Grammar ● 過去形

 We **visited** a Japanese garden. It **was** beautiful.
私たちは日本庭園を訪れました。それは美しかったです。

■ be 動詞の過去形は was / were を使って表します。

| 主語 | be動詞 | その他の情報 | 意味 |
|---|---|---|---|
| I / He / She | **was** | at home this morning. | 私/彼/彼女は今朝、家にいました。 |
| It | **was** | cold yesterday. | 昨日は寒かったです。 |
| We / You / They | **were** | busy last week. | 私たち/あなた（たち）/彼らは先週、忙しかったです。 |

[否定文] The movie **was not** [**wasn't**] exciting.　その映画は面白くありませんでした。
[疑問文] **Was** the weather good last weekend?　先週、天気はよかったですか。

■ 一般動詞の過去形には、規則変化するものと不規則変化するものがあります。
[規則変化] ask – ask**ed** / study – stud**ied** / stop – stop**ped** など
[不規則変化] eat – **ate** / go – **went** / take – **took** / know – **knew** など

| 主語 | 一般動詞 | その他の情報 | 意味 |
|---|---|---|---|
| My friend | **helped** | me with my homework. | 私の友人は宿題を手伝ってくれました。 |
| Mary | **had** | a good time at the party. | メアリーはパーティーで楽しい時間を過ごしました。 |

[否定文] You **didn't call** me last night.　あなたは昨晩私に電話しませんでした。
[疑問文] **Did** Jack **tell** you a lie?　ジャックはあなたに嘘をつきましたか。

I forgot my key again.

# Grammar Checking

**A** ( ) 内から正しい選択肢を選び、文を完成させましょう。

1. Masa ( **a.** works   **b.** is working   **c.** worked ) late last night.
2. We ( **a.** did   **b.** were   **c.** went ) to a movie after class.
3. ( **a.** Did David   **b.** Did David do   **c.** Did David did ) his homework?
4. Jack and Diane ( **a.** didn't   **b.** wasn't   **c.** weren't ) at the meeting this morning.
5. Albert Einstein ( **a.** alive   **b.** lived   **c.** was living ) from 1879 to 1955.
6. ( **a.** Is   **b.** Was   **c.** Were ) Mao at work yesterday?
7. My alarm clock didn't ( **a.** rang   **b.** ring   **c.** rung ) this morning.
8. I ( **a.** didn't have   **b.** didn't had   **c.** hadn't ) breakfast.

**B** 空所に適当な動詞を選択肢から選び、過去形にして書き入れましょう。

| enjoy | have | hear | leave | meet | pay |

1. Cathy _____ her umbrella on the train.
2. We _____ the soccer match very much.
3. I _____ a funny dream last night.
4. We _____ at the station and then walked to the restaurant together.
5. I _____ a strange noise outside my window last night.
6. Matt _____ for his new car in cash.

## Mission ! 2. 過去形を使ってみよう！

次の日本語を英語に直しましょう。

1. あなたがこの表を作成したのですか。            *表 chart

_____

2. ボブのプレゼンはとても興味深かったです。        *興味深い interesting

_____

## Reading

*Masa's Log*

**A** マサのインターン日記を読み、写真1〜4のうちマサが見たと書かれているものには○を、書かれていないものには×を入れましょう。　CheckLink　DL 17　CD 17

### MUNY

The first time I took the subway in New York, I saw some cool African hand-drummers. I went to see them perform the next day around the same time, but they weren't there. I later found out that they were Music Under New York (MUNY) approved performers, and they don't stay in one place. I checked their schedule on the MUNY website and saw them again a week later at a different location. Last week, I listened to a gospel singer, a guitarist and saxophone players.

*Note:* approved「認可された」

**1. (　　)**

**2. (　　)**

**3. (　　)**

**4. (　　)**

**B** 英文をもう一度読み、正しい選択肢を選びましょう。　CheckLink

1. MUNY means ( **a.** Music  **b.** Musicians ) Under New York.
2. Masa saw hand-drummers ( **a.** last week  **b.** the first time he took the subway ).
3. Masa found out the hand-drummers' schedule by ( **a.** asking them  **b.** looking on the MUNY website ).

## Wrap-Up Writing

**A** マサが先週の日曜にしたことについて、読んでみましょう。

**In the morning**
- eat bacon and eggs for breakfast
- do laundry

**In the afternoon**
- watch baseball on TV
- take a walk in Central Park

**In the evening**
- have a cup of tea
- read a book

**B** **A**の情報を文にまとめてみましょう。(　　　)には動詞の過去形を入れてください。

Last Sunday morning, Masa (　　　　　) _____ and eggs for breakfast and (　　　) laundry.  He watched _____ on TV and (　　　　　) a walk in Central Park in the afternoon.  In the evening, he (　　　　) a cup of _____ and (　　　　) a book.

**Mission** 3. あなた自身について書いてみよう！

**A**と**B**を参考にして、あなたが日曜の朝・昼・夜にしたことをそれぞれ書いてみましょう。

Last Sunday morning, I _____
_____
_____
_____

**Hints**  stay at home「家にいる」　do homework「宿題をする」　hang out with friends「友だちと遊ぶ」　work out at the gym「ジムで運動する」　take a bath「お風呂に入る」　read a comic book「漫画を読む」　set my alarm clock「アラームをセットする」　text my parents「両親にメールする」

# Unit 5 Hotel Guest Satisfaction

**Mission !**
- 相手を励ます
- 可算名詞・不可算名詞を理解する
- 大学で必要な物について書く

## Getting Ready

**A** 英語の意味に合う日本語を a〜e から選びましょう。

CheckLink　DL 18　CD 18

1. charming       (    )    a. 簡素な
2. comfortable    (    )    b. すてきな
3. fluffy         (    )    c. 狭い
4. plain          (    )    d. 心地よい
5. narrow         (    )    e. フカフカの

**B** マサが視察に訪れたホテルの一室のイラストを見ながら 1〜4 の英文を聞きましょう。イラストと合っていれば T、異なっていれば F を選びましょう。

CheckLink　DL 19　CD 19

1. T / F　　2. T / F　　3. T / F　　4. T / F

## Conversation

● *Lucky Lucy, Poor Masa*

ルーシーとマサは視察してきたホテルについて、上司のテッドに報告しています。

**A** 会話を聞きましょう。1～4について、聞き取った内容と合っていればT、異なっていればFを選びましょう。

1. Lucy's room was a little noisy. ( T / F )
2. Lucy liked her bath towel. ( T / F )
3. There was no air conditioner in Masa's room. ( T / F )
4. Masa enjoyed a long, hot shower. ( T / F )

**B** もう一度会話を聞いて、空所を埋めましょう。その後ペアになって、会話の練習をしましょう。

**Ted:** Lucy, tell me about your hotel.

**Lucy:** OK. The hotel was old and charming. My room was small, but very clean. There was very little (¹          ) from outside or from other (²          ). The room had a large (³          ). Oh, and the bath towel was big and fluffy.

**Ted:** I see. Masa?

**Masa:** My hotel was also quite old, but very plain. My room was small. There wasn't much (⁴          ) to walk around. The air (⁵          ) was noisy. The (⁶          ) didn't work well, and the (⁷          ) stayed hot for only a few (⁸          ). My bath towel was small and, umm, not fluffy.

**Lucy:** Poor Masa! Better luck next time!

### Mission  1. 相手を励ましてみよう！

ルーシーが励ましの言葉を述べている英文を探し、線を引きましょう。また、それを真似て次のセリフを言ってみましょう。

I hope _____ have better _____ next _____ !
次回はうまくいくように願っています。

Unit 5  Hotel Guest Satisfaction

## Breaking Down the Grammar ● 可算名詞・不可算名詞

**基本例文** I want **a hot dog**. I'll order **a cup of coffee**, too.
私はホットドッグが食べたいです。コーヒーも1杯頼もうと思います。

■ 英語の名詞には、数えられるもの（可算名詞）と数えられないもの（不可算名詞）があります。可算名詞の複数形は以下のように作ります。

| | |
|---|---|
| 語尾に s, es をつける | cat – cat**s** / room – room**s** / class – class**es** |
| 語尾を変えて -s/-es をつける | country – countr**ies** / leaf – lea**ves** |
| 不規則変化する | tooth – **teeth** / child – **children** / foot – **feet** |

[例] The **schoolchildren** take **classes** on Saturdays. 生徒たちは土曜に授業を受けます。
Kim bought five **knives** and ten **forks**. キムはナイフ5本とフォーク10本を買いました。

■ 不可算名詞には s はつきませんが、数量や単位を表す語句を使って数量を表します。

| 種類 | 例 | 数量、集合体を表す表現 |
|---|---|---|
| 物質名詞 | sugar（砂糖）、meat（肉）、milk（牛乳）、money（お金） | **some** money　いくらかのお金<br>**a glass of** milk　グラス1杯の牛乳 |
| 抽象名詞 | time（時間）、love（愛情）、anger（怒り）、information（情報）、advice（助言） | **a lot of** love　たくさんの愛情<br>**some** advice　いくつかの助言<br>**a little** time　少しの時間 |
| 集合名詞 | furniture（家具）、baggage（手荷物）、police（警察） | **a piece of** furniture　1つの家具<br>**the police**　（集合体・組織としての）警察 |

■ 数量を表す表現として、a few / few と a little / little もよく使われます。few は可算名詞に、little は不可算名詞につきます。

There are **a few students** in the computer room.
PC教室に2～3人の学生がいます。

We had very **little rain** last month.
先月はほとんど雨が降りませんでした。

You have a beautiful eye.

# Grammar Checking

**A** (　　) 内から正しい選択肢を選び、文を完成させましょう。

1. Do you like ( **a.** vegetable　**b.** a vegetable　**c.** vegetables )?
2. Carl takes his coffee with ( **a.** milk　**b.** a milk　**c.** milks ).
3. I don't have ( **a.** many　**b.** much　**c.** few ) money in the bank.
4. Charlotte has ( **a.** long hair　**b.** long hairs　**c.** a long hair ).
5. I need ( **a.** an information　**b.** some information　**c.** many information ), please.
6. I don't know much French — only ( **a.** little　**b.** a little　**c.** a few ) words.
7. Hurry up. We don't have ( **a.** little　**b.** few　**c.** much ) time.
8. It's rainy today. There are ( **a.** few　**b.** little　**c.** a little ) people in the park.

**B** 例にならって英文中の間違いを含む部分に線を引き、[　]内に正しく書き直しましょう。

1. **A:** Do you have a car?
   **B:** No, but I have ~~some~~ driver's license.　→ [ a ]
2. **A:** Does Pam eat meats?　→ [ 　 ]
   **B:** Yes, but only chickens.　→ [ 　 ]
3. **A:** Ten person are on this tour.　→ [ 　 ]
   **B:** Are there any child?　→ [ 　 ]
4. **A:** There are little students here.　→ [ 　 ]
   **B:** Yes, it's small class today.　→ [ 　 ]
5. **A:** Here, have cup of coffee.　→ [ 　 ]
   **B:** Thanks. Do you have some sugars?　→ [ 　 ]

## Mission　2. 可算名詞・不可算名詞に注意して書いてみよう！

次の日本語を英語に直しましょう。

1. 今日はあまりたくさんのお金を持っていません。

2. 箱の中に３切れのピザがあります。

# Reading

*Masa's Log*

**A** マサのインターン日記「ホテルでの必需品調査」を読み、写真a〜dのアイテムを人気の順に並べ替えましょう。　CheckLink　DL 21　CD 21

### Business Traveler Hotel Room Wish List

I did some research about what business travelers want in their hotel rooms. The first thing they want is fast, free WiFi. Slow Internet is the number one complaint of hotel guests. Second, they want easy-to-find electrical outlets to charge their laptop computers and mobile phones. The third item is a work desk. Next is plenty of bottled water in the mini fridge. Businesspeople don't like to leave their rooms to buy it. Another item that businesspeople often want in their hotel rooms is an iron.

*Notes:* complaint「苦情」　electrical outlet「電源、コンセント」　fridge「冷蔵庫」

¹(　　) ➡ ²(　　) ➡ ³(　　) ➡ ⁴(　　)

**B** 英文をもう一度読み、正しい選択肢を選びましょう。　CheckLink

1. The number one complaint of business travelers is ( **a.** slow Internet　**b.** no Internet ) in their hotel room.
2. Businesspeople don't like to leave their rooms to get ( **a.** snacks　**b.** water ).
3. Business travelers often want ( **a.** fast room service　**b.** an iron ).

## Wrap-Up Writing

**A** 先月プリーズトラベル社が注文したオフィス用品の注文票を読んでみましょう。

| Order Form | | |
|---|---|---|
| Item | Quantity | Unit |
| Scissors | 2 | pair |
| Paper | 3 | box |
| Notebook | 7 | - |
| Clipboard | 2 | - |
| Iced coffee | 5 | carton |
| Mineral water | 20 | bottle |

*Note:* quantity「数量」

**B** **A** の情報を文にまとめてみましょう。

Please Travel ordered two _____ of _____, three _____ of paper, _____ notebooks, two clipboards, five cartons _____ iced _____ and _____ _____ of mineral water.

### Mission  3. あなた自身について書いてみよう！

**A** と **B** を参考にして、あなたが大学の授業で必要な文具やその他の用具について書いてみましょう。6点挙げ、それぞれ必要な数も書いてください。

I need the following supplies for my classes:

① _____   ② _____

③ _____   ④ _____

⑤ _____   ⑥ _____

**Hints**   mechanical pencil「シャープペン」   ruler「定規」   dictionary「辞書」

# Unit 6 Brainstorming

**Mission**
- これからすることを提案する
- 進行形の使い方に慣れる
- 健康状態について書く

## Getting Ready

**A** 英語の意味に合う日本語を a～e から選びましょう。

CheckLink　DL 22　CD 22

1. awake　　　　（　）　　a. パンフレット
2. daydream　　（　）　　b. 目標に定める
3. brochure　　 （　）　　c. 提案
4. suggestion　 （　）　　d. 空想する、夢想する
5. target　　　　（　）　　e. 目が覚めて

**B** PCに向かって話しているマサとルーシーのイラストを見ながら 1～4 の英文を聞きましょう。イラストと合っていればT、異なっていればFを選びましょう。

CheckLink　DL 23　CD 23

1. T / F　　2. T / F　　3. T / F　　4. T / F

## Conversation  ● Deep in Thought

マサとルーシーは仕事で出された課題について、互いに意見を出し合っています。

**A** 会話を聞きましょう。1～4について、聞き取った内容と合っていればT、異なっていればFを選びましょう。

CheckLink  DL 24  CD 24

1. Masa was sleeping. ( T / F )
2. Masa is making a shopping list. ( T / F )
3. The brochure is for young families. ( T / F )
4. Masa suggests talking to some children. ( T / F )

**B** もう一度会話を聞いて、空所を埋めましょう。その後ペアになって、会話の練習をしましょう。

Lucy: Masa? …Masa? …Are you (¹           )? …Masa! …MASA!!!
Masa: Huh? …No, I'm awake.
Lucy: (²           ) you daydreaming?
Masa: No, I (³           ) daydreaming. I was (⁴           ) of ideas for the travel brochure.
Lucy: Great! Are you (⁵           ) them down?
Masa: Yeah, I'm (⁶           ) a list of interesting places to visit in New York. Do you have any suggestions?
Lucy: Well, (⁷           ) targeting couples with young children. Hmm… let me think…
Masa: I know! Let's go to Central Park and talk to some kids. …Lucy? …Lucy? …Are you (⁸           )? …Lucy! …LUCY!!!

## Mission  1. 相手に提案してみよう！

マサがルーシーにこれから行く場所を提案している英文を探し、線を引きましょう。また、それを真似て次のセリフを言ってみましょう。

Let's _____ Anne and _____ her to the party.
アンに電話してパーティーに招待しよう。

Unit 6  Brainstorming  45

# Breaking Down the Grammar

● 進行形

  Ben **is texting** his girlfriend now.
ベンは今、彼女に携帯メールを送っています。

■ 現在あるいは過去のある時点で進行中の動作を表す場合や、習慣的に行っていることを表す場合、進行形を使います。

| 主語 | be動詞＋<br>一般動詞の-ing形 | その他の情報 | 意味 |
| --- | --- | --- | --- |
| Sam | **is listening** | to music in his room. | サムは自分の部屋で音楽を聞いています。 |
| Some people | **are doing** | yoga in the park. | 何人かの人々が公園でヨガをしています。 |
| We | **were studying** | in the library this morning. | 私たちは今朝、図書館で勉強していました。 |
| Josh | **was** always **wearing** | a funny T-shirt. | ジョシュはいつも面白いＴシャツを着ていました。 |

▶習慣的に行っていることを表すとき、always「いつも」やoften「よく」などの副詞を使います。

［否定文］ We **aren't taking** any photos. 私たちは写真を撮っていません。
［疑問文］ **Are** you **drinking** green tea? あなたは今緑茶を飲んでいますか。

■ 現在進行形は、近い未来の予定を表すときにも使われます。
 I **am seeing** a dentist at 10:00 tomorrow. 明日の10時に歯医者に行く予定です。

■ 状態を表す動詞（like / believe / know など）は基本的に進行形になりません。
 × I am liking oranges.
 ○ I **like** oranges. 私はオレンジが好きです。

# Grammar Checking

**A** (　　) 内から正しい選択肢を選び、文を完成させましょう。

1. Jane ( **a.** does   **b.** is   **c.** was ) studying now.
2. Listen! Someone ( **a.** cries   **b.** is cried   **c.** is crying ).
3. Ted and Patty ( **a.** are having   **b.** is having   **c.** were having ) a meeting then.
4. I ( **a.** am starting   **b.** am start   **c.** was starting ) a new job next week.
5. ( **a.** Was   **b.** Were   **c.** Are ) you sleeping at 10:00 last night?
6. ( **a.** Are playing the boys   **b.** Are the boys playing   **c.** The boys is playing ) now?
7. Sorry, I didn't see you. ( **a.** I'm   **b.** I'm not   **c.** I wasn't ) wearing my glasses then.
8. No one ( **a.** was   **b.** were   **c.** wasn't ) watching TV, so I turned it off.

**B** (　　) 内の語句を並べ替えて、日本語に合う文を作りましょう。

1. ( party / enjoying / the / you / are )　パーティーを楽しんでいますか。
   _____?

2. ( very / team / well / playing / the / isn't )　そのチームはあまり上手にプレーしていません。
   _____.

3. ( to / students / teacher / their / weren't / the / listening )
   学生たちは先生の話を聞いていませんでした。
   _____.

4. ( seat / but / excuse / my / sitting / me, / in / you're )
   すみませんが、あなたは私の席に座っています。
   _____.

## Mission　2. 現在進行形と過去進行形を使ってみよう！

次の日本語を英語に直しましょう。

1. あなたはコンタクトレンズをしていますか。　　　＊コンタクトレンズ contact lenses

2. 今日彼女はズボンをはいていますが、昨日はスカートをはいていました。　＊ズボン pants

# Reading

*Masa's Log*

**A** マサのインターン日記を読み、イラスト1〜4のうちマサがしたと書かれていることには○を、書かれていないものには×を入れましょう。 CheckLink　DL 25　CD 25

### Mind Your Body Language

I'm learning a lot about business and body language. Here are some examples. Once I was shaking hands with Ted. He said, "Shake firmly, Masa. Your hand feels like a dead fish! A strong handshake means a strong businessperson. And don't look down. Eye contact shows you're honest." Another time I was listening to Patty with my arms crossed. She said, "Crossing your arms means you're impatient." Then I was tapping my fingers. She said, "You're not paying attention, are you?" She was right.

1. (　　)
2. (　　)
3. (　　)
4. (　　)

**B** 英文をもう一度読み、正しい選択肢を選びましょう。　CheckLink

1. Ted thought Masa's handshake felt ( **a.** wet　**b.** weak ).
2. Eye contact is a sign of ( **a.** power　**b.** honesty ).
3. Tapping your fingers means you ( **a.** are not listening carefully　**b.** don't believe the person ).

# Wrap-Up Writing

**A** 最近体調を崩しがちなマサは病院に行ってみることにしました。マサが答えた問診票を読んでみましょう。

### Lifestyle Questions

Name: Masahiro Nakata

Recently, are you ...

(1) ... getting more than 7 hours of sleep a night?  Yes /(No)
(2) ... having breakfast every morning?  (Yes)/ No
(3) ... eating lots of fruit and vegetables?  Yes /(No)
(4) ... exercising for more than 15 minutes every day?  (Yes)/ No
(5) ... feeling stressed out from work or school?  Yes /(No)

**B** **A** の情報を文にまとめてみましょう。

Recently, Masa _____ sleeping more than 7 hours a night.  He _____ _____ breakfast every morning.  He _____ _____ a lot of fruit and vegetables.  He _____ _____ for more than 15 minutes a day.  He _____ _____ stressed out from work.

**Mission** 3. あなた自身について書いてみよう！

あなた自身について**A**の問診票に答えた後、**B**を参考にしてあなたの健康状態について書いてみましょう。

Recently, I _____ a night.

_____

_____

_____

Unit 6  Brainstorming

# Unit 7

# Glad to Be of Service

**Mission**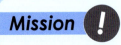
- 助けを求める
- WH疑問文の使い方に慣れる
- 好きな人物を紹介する

## Getting Ready

**A** 英語の意味に合う日本語を a〜e から選びましょう。

CheckLink　DL 26　CD 26

1. terrific　　　（　）　　a. 札入れ、財布
2. wallet　　　（　）　　b. 中に
3. possible　　（　）　　c. 革の
4. leather　　　（　）　　d. すばらしい
5. inside　　　（　）　　e. 可能な

**B** 接客業務中のマサのイラストを見ながら 1〜4 の質問文と応答を聞きましょう。応答がイラストと合っていれば T、異なっていれば F を選びましょう。

CheckLink　DL 27　CD 27

1. T / F　　2. T / F　　3. T / F　　4. T / F

## Conversation  ● *I Lost My Wallet*

マサはパティに見守られながら、落とし物を探しに来たお客さんに応対しています。

**A** 会話を聞きましょう。1〜4について、聞き取った内容と合っていればT、異なっていればFを選びましょう。

1. The man's name is William.  ( T / F )
2. The man's wallet is brown.  ( T / F )
3. The man lost his credit cards.  ( T / F )
4. A few hundred dollars were in the wallet.  ( T / F )

**B** もう一度会話を聞いて、空所を埋めましょう。その後ペアになって、会話の練習をしましょう。

**Masa:** Mr. and Mrs. Williams. Hi! (¹          ) was your tour?
**Man:** Terrific, but I lost my wallet. Is it possible for you to help me find it?
**Masa:** Yes, of course. (²       ) (³       ) (⁴       ) wallet is it?
**Man:** It's a brown leather wallet.
**Masa:** And (⁵        ) was inside?
**Man:** Just money. My wife keeps our credit cards in her purse.
**Masa:** OK. (⁶       ) (⁷       ) (⁸       ) was in it?
**Man:** About 300 dollars. …Oh, and there's a picture of my wife and me inside.
**Masa:** A picture… Hmmm…
**Patty:** Are you wearing chicken costumes in the picture? We got a call from the bus company this morning. They have your wallet.

### Mission  1. 相手に助けを求めてみよう！

お客さんがマサに助けを求めている英文を探し、線を引きましょう。また、それを真似て次のセリフを言ってみましょう。

Is _____ possible for you to _____ me _____ this box?
この箱を運ぶのを手伝っていただけますか。

# Breaking Down the Grammar ● WH疑問文

 **What** do you do?

あなたは（仕事として）何をしていますか。／職業は何ですか。

■「誰／何／いつ／どこ」などの情報をたずねる疑問文では、疑問詞を使います。

| 疑問詞 | 例文 |
|---|---|
| **who**<br>誰 | **Who** were you talking to? あなたは誰と話していたのですか。<br>**Who** broke this toy? 誰がこのおもちゃを壊したのですか。<br>▶「誰が〜しますか」とたずねるときは、Who の直後に動詞が来ます。 |
| **what**<br>何 | **What** do you usually eat for breakfast?<br>あなたは普段朝食に何を食べますか。<br>**What** kind of music does your father like?<br>あなたのお父さんは何の音楽が好きですか。 |
| **when**<br>いつ | **When** is your birthday? あなたの誕生日はいつですか。<br>**When** did the meeting finish? 会議はいつ終わったのですか。 |
| **where**<br>どこ | **Where** did you go last weekend?<br>あなたは先週末どこへ行きましたか。 |
| **how**<br>どのように・<br>どのくらい | **How** much is this camera? このカメラはいくらですか。<br>**How** often do you play tennis?<br>あなたはどのくらい頻繁にテニスをしますか。<br>▶ How はさまざまな形容詞や副詞と結びついて「どのくらい〜？」とたずねます。<br>　How long「どのくらいの期間」、How tall「どのくらいの高さ」など |
| **why**<br>なぜ | **Why** did you choose Bali for your honeymoon?<br>なぜあなたは新婚旅行にバリを選んだのですか。 |
| **which**<br>どちら | **Which** way is the hospital, this way **or** that way?<br>病院に行くには、この道とあの道のどちらですか。 |

Who's that handsome guy?

## Grammar Checking

**A** (　) 内から正しい選択肢を選び、文を完成させましょう。　　CheckLink

1. ( **a.** What old　**b.** How age　**c.** How old ) are you?
2. ( **a.** What　**b.** Where　**c.** Who ) did you go for dinner last night?
3. Where ( **a.** are you　**b.** do you　**c.** you are ) from?
4. When ( **a.** starts the meeting　**b.** does the meeting start　**c.** the meeting starts )?
5. How ( **a.** long　**b.** far　**c.** much ) did you stay in Hawaii?
6. ( **a.** How　**b.** Where　**c.** Which ) tour do you want to take?
7. Why ( **a.** were you late　**b.** you were late　**c.** did you late ) this morning?
8. How ( **a.** often do you　**b.** you do often　**c.** often you do ) go shopping?

**B** 例にならって、次の英文の下線部をたずねる疑問文を作りましょう。

1. **a.** <u>Mike</u> broke the cup.　　Who broke the cup?

    **b.** Mike broke <u>the cup</u>.　　_____

2. **a.** <u>The meeting</u> starts at 6:00.　　_____

    **b.** The meeting starts <u>at 6:00</u>.　　_____

3. **a.** Masa went <u>to the park</u> on Sunday.　　_____

    **b.** Masa went to the park <u>on Sunday</u>.　　_____

### Mission ❗ 2. 疑問詞を使って質問文を作ってみよう！

次の日本語を英語に直しましょう。

1. あなたは今日いくつの授業がありますか。

    _____

2. あなたは会社の前で誰と話していましたか。　　＊～の前で in front of ～

    _____

Unit 7　Glad to Be of Service

# Reading

● *Masa's Log*

**A** マサのインターン日記を読み、イラスト a〜d を実際に起きた順に並べ替えましょう。

CheckLink　DL 29　CD 29

## A Very Unusual Customer Request

Patty once received a very unusual customer request. What was the request? The customer wanted to camp in the HOT Sahara Desert in August — in an air-conditioned tent! How hot does it get in August? Only fifty-five degrees Celcius! ☺ How did Patty manage? She bought a generator and air conditioner and sent them by truck to the camping area. A worker then connected the generator to the air conditioner. The customer turned on the air conditioner — and left it on HIGH the whole time.

¹(　　) ➡ ²(　　) ➡ ³(　　) ➡ ⁴(　　)

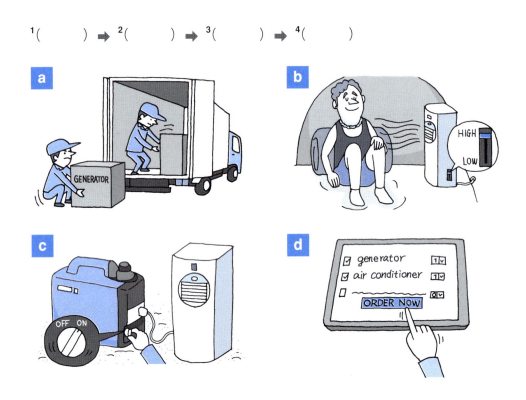

**B** 英文をもう一度読み、正しい選択肢を選びましょう。　CheckLink

1. The customer wanted to camp ( **a.** on the beach　**b.** in the desert ).
2. The customer wanted to go camping ( **a.** in July　**b.** in August ).
3. The temperature reaches ( **a.** 45℃　**b.** 55℃ ) at that time of year.

## Wrap-Up Writing

**A** 好きな親戚についてマサが書いた文章を読んでみましょう。

One of my favorite relatives is my ¹grandfather. My grandfather's name is ²Toshio. He is very ³kind and friendly. He is about ⁴70 years old. He lives in ⁵Osaka. I last saw him around ⁶a year ago.

**B** (　　) 内の語句を並べ替え、**A** の下線部をたずねる疑問文を作りましょう。

1. ( is / favorite / your / who / relatives / of / one )
   _____?
2. ( name / grandfather's / is / what / your ) _____?
3. ( he / of / is / person / kind / what ) _____?
4. ( old / he / is / how ) _____?
5. ( does / live / where / he ) _____?
6. ( him / when / did / last / you / see ) _____?

### Mission ❗ 3. あなた自身について書いてみよう！

**A** と **B** を参考にして、あなたが好きな親戚あるいは有名人について書いてみましょう。

One of my favorite _____

_____

_____

_____

**Hints**
celebrity「有名人」　aunt「おばさん」　uncle「おじさん」　cousin「いとこ」　niece「めい」
nephew「おい」　funny「愉快な」　caring「思いやりのある」　loving「愛情深い」
reliable「頼りがいのある」　talented「才能のある」　handsome「ハンサムな」

# Unit 8  Socializing with Co-Workers

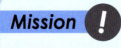

- パーティーに誘う
- 動名詞・不定詞を理解する
- 好きなこと・嫌いなことについて書く

## Getting Ready

**A** 英語の意味に合う日本語を a〜e から選びましょう。

1. food cart       (   )    a. 持ち寄りパーティー
2. potluck party   (   )    b. 分け合う
3. dish            (   )    c. ビュッフェ
4. share           (   )    d. 料理
5. buffet          (   )    e. 屋台

**B** ランチ休憩中のマサとパティのイラストを見ながら 1〜4 の英文を聞きましょう。イラストと合っていれば T、異なっていれば F を選びましょう。

1. T / F    2. T / F    3. T / F    4. T / F

# Conversation

● A Party Invitation

ホットドッグを食べながら、パティは何やら楽しそうな計画を教えてくれました。

**A** 会話を聞きましょう。1〜4について、聞き取った内容と合っていればT、異なっていればFを選びましょう。

1. Masa likes food carts. ( T / F )
2. Masa will go to the office party this Friday night. ( T / F )
3. A potluck is a kind of soup. ( T / F )
4. Masa will make something for the party. ( T / F )

**B** もう一度会話を聞いて、空所を埋めましょう。その後ペアになって、会話の練習をしましょう。

**Masa:** I really like these food carts. And I really like (¹         )!
**Patty:** Yeah, me too. Speaking of eating, we decided to (²         ) a potluck party at our office this Friday night. Do you want to come?
**Masa:** I'd love to (³         )! …Umm, what's a potluck party?
**Patty:** Everyone brings a different dish. And then we share the food and enjoy (⁴         ) dinner and (⁵         ). It's like a buffet.
**Masa:** That sounds nice, but…
**Patty:** …But what?
**Masa:** Well, I never learned to (⁶         ). I prefer (⁷         ) to restaurants.
**Patty:** Don't worry. You don't need to (⁸         ) anything. Just buy something.
**Masa:** Oh, OK. Whew!

## Mission  1. 相手を誘ってみよう！

パティがマサをパーティーに誘っている英文を探し、線を引きましょう。また、それを真似て次のセリフを言ってみましょう。

Do you _____ to come _____ our graduation _____?
私たちの卒業パーティーに来ない？

## Breaking Down the Grammar　●動名詞・不定詞

**基本例文**　I **decided to work** at a travel agency.
私は旅行代理店で働くことを決めました。

■「留学することを決める」のように、1つの文中で2つ以上の動詞を使う場合、動名詞（-ing）や不定詞（to＋動詞の原形）を使います。

■後ろに動名詞が来る動詞：enjoy, dislike, finish, keep, mind, practiceなど

| 主語＋一般動詞 | 動名詞 | その他の情報 | 意味 |
|---|---|---|---|
| We enjoyed | swimming | in the lake. | 私たちは湖で泳ぐことを楽しみました。 |

▶「現在あるいはこれまでに起こったことに対して何かする」動詞が多い

■後ろに不定詞が来る動詞：want, hope, need, decide, plan, pretend, promiseなど

| 主語＋一般動詞 | 不定詞 | その他の情報 | 意味 |
|---|---|---|---|
| Aki wants | to work | abroad. | アキは海外で働きたいと思っています。 |
| I promise | to be | here by 7:00 tomorrow. | 私は明日の朝7時までにここに来ることを約束します。 |

▶「あることをしようとする意欲や意図を表す」動詞が多い

■どちらでもよい動詞：start, begin, love, like, preferなど
It started **snowing** / **to snow** an hour ago.　1時間前に雪が降り始めました。

■不定詞か動名詞のどちらが来るかで意味が変わる動詞：forget, remember, tryなど
Remember **to turn** off the air conditioner.　エアコンを消すのを忘れないでね。
I remember **turning** off the air conditioner this morning.
今朝エアコンを消したことを覚えています。

He tried to steal my purse.

58

## Grammar Checking

**A** (　　) 内から正しい選択肢を選び、文を完成させましょう。aとbのどちらも当てはまる場合はc. *both*を選んでください。

1. Maki enjoys ( **a.** playing    **b.** to play    **c.** *both* ) tennis.
2. I hope ( **a.** finishing    **b.** to finish    **c.** *both* ) my report tonight.
3. It started ( **a.** raining    **b.** to rain    **c.** *both* ) a few minutes ago.
4. We like ( **a.** going    **b.** to go    **c.** *both* ) to the beach in summer.
5. The boss wants ( **a.** having    **b.** to have    **c.** *both* ) a meeting now.
6. Did you finish ( **a.** watching    **b.** to watch    **c.** *both* ) the DVD?
7. I decided ( **a.** changing    **b.** to change    **c.** *both* ) jobs.
8. I don't mind ( **a.** taking    **b.** to take    **c.** *both* ) the bus to work.

**B** 空所に適当な動詞を選択肢から選び、動名詞または不定詞にして書き入れましょう。

| buy | find | make | speak | take | watch |

1. Don't forget _____ some milk at the supermarket.
2. Our team keeps _____ the same mistakes.
3. I'm tired. I want _____ a rest.
4. Sara really dislikes _____ sports.
5. Let's practice _____ English together.
6. I don't have any money. I need _____ an ATM.

### Mission  2. 動名詞と不定詞を使ってみよう！

次の日本語を英語に直しましょう。

1. 今年の夏はカナダに行く計画を立てています。　　　　　　＊計画を立てる  plan

_____

2. マリは先月運転の講習を受け始めました。　　　　　　＊運転の講習  driving lessons

_____

# Reading

● *Masa's Log*

**A** マサのインターン日記を読み、写真1〜4の食べ物のおおよその価格を選択肢から選びましょう。

## New York Food Carts

I enjoy eating and I like to try different things. However, I hate cooking and I don't have much money. Luckily, New York has about 5,000 food carts, with all kinds of tasty and inexpensive food! In general, a hot dog costs $2, curry and rice is $5, and Asian rice noodles are $4. A large donut and coffee are about $3. Is the food safe to eat? Yes, I think so. Vendors require a license, and they need to take a health and safety class.

1. (  )
2. (  )
3. (  )
4. (  )

a. $2    b. $3    c. $4    d. $5

**B** 英文をもう一度読み、正しい選択肢を選びましょう。

1. Masa ( **a.** often cooks   **b.** hates cooking ).
2. There are about ( **a.** 500   **b.** 5,000 ) food carts in New York.
3. Vendors need to take a ( **a.** fire safety   **b.** health and safety ) class.

## Wrap-Up Writing

**A** マサがプリーズトラベル社でのさまざまな仕事について答えたアンケートを読んでみましょう。

### Work Preferences

**1** = like / enjoy   **2** = don't mind   **3** = don't really like / dislike

- attend meetings        [ 1 ② 3 ]
- clean the office       [ 1 2 ③ ]
- meet customers         [ ① 2 3 ]
- talk with co-workers   [ ① 2 3 ]
- work overtime          [ 1 ② 3 ]
- answer the phone       [ 1 2 ③ ]

**Notes:** attend「出席する」  work overtime「残業する」

**B** **A** の情報を文にまとめてみましょう。

Masa likes to talk with co-workers, and he enjoys _____ _____.

He doesn't mind _____ meetings or _____ overtime. He doesn't

really like _____ the office, and he dislikes _____ the phone.

### Mission  3. あなた自身について書いてみよう！

**A** と **B** を参考にして、あなたが大学生活の中で好きなこと・あまり好きではないこと・嫌いなことについて書いてみましょう。

I like to _____

I enjoy _____

I don't mind _____

I dislike _____

**Hints** talk with friends「友だちと話す」  participate in club activities「クラブ活動をする」  talk with my teachers after class「授業後に先生と話をする」  have class discussions「授業で議論をする」  do assignments「課題に取り組む」  have morning classes「朝の授業に出る」  memorize many things「多くのことを暗記する」  make presentations「プレゼンをする」

# Unit 9 Vacation Spots

**Mission**
- 相手に約束する
- 未来形の使い方に慣れる
- 未来の自分について書く

## Getting Ready

**A** 英語の意味に合う日本語を a～e から選びましょう。

CheckLink　DL 34　CD 34

1. on the way　　　(　)　　a. 国立公園
2. national park　　(　)　　b. 滝
3. falls　　　　　　(　)　　c. 見せ場
4. overnight　　　 (　)　　d. 途中で
5. highlight　　　　(　)　　e. 泊まりがけで

**B** バス停にいるマサたちと周囲の様子を描いたイラストを見ながら1～4の英文を聞きましょう。イラストと合っていればT、異なっていればFを選びましょう。

CheckLink　DL 35　CD 35

1. T / F　　2. T / F　　3. T / F　　4. T / F

## Conversation  ● Tour Talk

マサは来るツアー添乗に向けて、パティとバス乗り場で打ち合わせをしています。

**A** 会話を聞きましょう。1〜4について、聞き取った内容と合っていればT、異なっていればFを選びましょう。

CheckLink　DL 36　CD 36

1. The tour starts at 7:30.　　　　　　　　　　( T / F )
2. They will arrive at Niagara Falls late at night.　( T / F )
3. They're going to stay in Canada for one night.　( T / F )
4. Patty says the illumination of the falls is the best part of the tour.
　　　　　　　　　　　　　　　　　　　　　　( T / F )

**B** もう一度会話を聞いて、空所を埋めましょう。その後ペアになって、会話の練習をしましょう。

**Patty:** The tour starts at 7:30 a.m. You and I will (¹　　　　　) here at 6:30.
**Masa:** OK, I promise I won't be late.
**Patty:** Now, on the way to Niagara Falls, (²　　　　　) visit a national park.
**Masa:** What time (³　　　　　) we arrive at Niagara Falls?
**Patty:** Around 6 p.m. Everyone will (⁴　　　　　) free time to walk around and enjoy the colorful illumination of the falls.
**Masa:** (⁵　　　　　) we also (⁶　　　　　) to go to the Canadian side of the falls?
**Patty:** Yes, we're going (⁷　　　　　) stay overnight on the Canadian side. The next morning is the highlight of the tour. We'll (⁸　　　　　) a boat cruise and go very close to the falls.
**Masa:** Not *over* the falls, I hope!

### Mission ❗ 1. 相手に約束してみよう！

マサが遅れずに来ることを約束している英文を探し、線を引きましょう。また、それを真似て次のセリフを言ってみましょう。

　　I _____ I will always _____ _____.
　　どんなときもあなたを助けると約束します。

Unit 9　Vacation Spots

## Breaking Down the Grammar　●未来形

**基本例文** My friend **will** work as an intern at the airport.
私の友人は空港でインターンとして働くでしょう。

■ 未来のことを表すとき、will や be going to を使います。「（これから）〜します」と意思を伝える場合や、「〜するでしょう」と未来について予想する場合は、will を使います。

| 主語 | will＋動詞の原形 | その他の情報 | 意味 |
| --- | --- | --- | --- |
| I | **will** stay | here until 5:00. | 私は5時までここにいます。 |
| Lisa | **will** get | the promotion. | リサは昇格するでしょう。 |

■ 確定している予定を表す場合は、be going to を使います。

| 主語 | be動詞＋going to ＋動詞の原形 | その他の情報 | 意味 |
| --- | --- | --- | --- |
| We | **are going to** work | in the same office. | 私たちは同じ事務所で働く予定です。 |
| Sam | **is going to** take | a Spanish course this semester. | サムは今学期、スペイン語の授業を履修する予定です。 |

［否定文］

I **will not** [**won't**] bother you anymore.　私はこれ以上あなたに迷惑をかけません。
I **will never** see him again.　私は今後彼に会うことは決してないでしょう。
This **is not going to** be an easy job.　これは簡単な仕事にはならないでしょう。

［疑問文］

**Will** you apply for this job?
あなたはこの仕事に応募しますか。

**Is it going to** rain this afternoon?
今日の午後、雨は降りますか。

Where **are you going to** stay in Hokkaido?
あなたは北海道のどこに滞在する予定ですか。

Everything's OK. I'll be out in a minute.

# Grammar Checking

**A** (　) 内から正しい選択肢を選び、文を完成させましょう。

1. The meeting ( **a.** will　**b.** will be　**c.** is going ) start at 3:00.
2. ( **a.** We'll　**b.** We going　**c.** We're going ) to watch the game tonight.
3. ( **a.** You will　**b.** Are you going　**c.** Will you ) to go to Jack's party?
4. Sorry, ( **a.** I'll　**b.** I'm going to　**c.** I won't ) have time to meet you today.
5. We ( **a.** will　**b.** are going　**c.** will going ) to drive to the lake on Sunday.
6. Ed and Sue are going ( **a.** to marriage　**b.** to married　**c.** to get married )!
7. Where ( **a.** you will be　**b.** will be you　**c.** will you be ) this afternoon?
8. ( **a.** Will this train stop　**b.** Is going to stop this train　**c.** Are this train going to stop ) at the next station?

**B** (　) 内の語句を並べ替えて、日本語に合う文を作りましょう。

1. ( dinner / going / Paul / cook / is / to )　今夜はポールが夕食を作ります。
   _____ tonight.

2. ( me / not / she / to / will / speak )　彼女は私に話しかけようとしません。
   _____.

3. ( much / lunch / for / time / have / won't )　私にはランチの時間があまりないでしょう。
   I _____.

4. ( buy / are / that / going / you / computer / to )　あのパソコンを買うつもりですか。
   _____?

## Mission ❗ 2. 未来形を使ってみよう！

次の日本語を英語に直しましょう。

1. 私は今夜顧客に会う予定です。　　　　　　　　　　＊顧客　a customer
   _____

2. 私はあなたにハワイからハガキを送るでしょう。　　＊ハガキ　a postcard
   _____

# Reading

● Masa's Log

**A** マサのインターン日記を読み、1〜4の各項目について内容と一致するほうのイラストを選びましょう。

CheckLink  DL 37  CD 37

## Weekend Travel Plans

Jim from Please Travel invited me to Lake Placid for the weekend. Lake Placid is about 460 km north of New York. Jim says it will take about five hours by car. We're going to stay with Jim's parents. They own a cabin by the lake. It's going to be a quiet and relaxing weekend. We're going to sit on the deck, have a barbecue, go fishing and play golf. I look forward to getting out of the city for a few days.

**1.** プラシッド湖の位置

a

b

**2.** 交通手段

a

b

**3.** 宿泊する場所

a

b

**4.** 予定しているアクティビティ

a

b

**B** 英文をもう一度読み、正しい選択肢を選びましょう。

CheckLink

1. Masa will be in Lake Placid for ( **a.** a couple of days   **b.** a week ).
2. It will take about ( **a.** three   **b.** five ) hours to get to Lake Placid.
3. Masa and Jim will play ( **a.** golf   **b.** tennis ) there.

## Wrap-Up Writing

**A** マサが15年後の未来について答えたアンケートを読んでみましょう。

### Imagine what your life will be like 15 years from now.

- What will your job be? — cabin attendant
- Are you going to live in a house or an apartment? — house
- Where are you going to live? — Tokyo
- Will you be married or single? — married
- Will you have any children? — Yes, 4 ( 2 boys & 2 girls )
- Will you have a pet? What kind? — no pets

**B** **A** の情報を文にまとめてみましょう。

Fifteen years from now, Masa _____ be a _____ attendant. He _____ going _____ live in a _____ in Tokyo. He will _____ married with four _____ — two boys and two _____. He _____ have a pet.

### Mission ! 3. あなた自身について書いてみよう！

**A** と **B** を参考にして、あなたの15年後の理想の生活について書いてみましょう。

Fifteen years from now, I will be _____

_____

_____

_____

**Hints**
tour conductor「ツアーコンダクター」　salaried worker「サラリーマン」　homemaker「主婦」
nurse「看護師」　restaurant owner「レストラン経営者」　my hometown「故郷の町」
a pet cat「ペットのネコ」　a hamster「ハムスター」

Unit 9　Vacation Spots

# Unit 10 Sports Talk

**Mission**
- 好みを伝える
- 比較級・最上級を理解する
- 自分の価値観について書く

## Getting Ready

**A** 英語の意味に合う日本語を a〜e から選びましょう。

CheckLink　DL 38　CD 38

1. especially　（　）　　a. 有名な
2. famous　　　（　）　　b. 男の人
3. windy　　　 （　）　　c. 伝統的な
4. traditional　（　）　　d. 特に
5. guy　　　　 （　）　　e. 風の強い

**B** ニューヨークのヤンキースタジアムで野球観戦をするマサたちのイラストを見ながら1〜4の英文を聞きましょう。イラストと合っていればT、異なっていればFを選びましょう。

CheckLink　DL 39　CD 39

1. T / F　　2. T / F　　3. T / F　　4. T / F

## Conversation

● At Yankee Stadium

野球観戦に来たテッド、マサ、ルーシーは、スポーツ談義で盛り上がっています。

**A** 会話を聞きましょう。1〜4について、聞き取った内容と合っていればT、異なっていればFを選びましょう。

CheckLink　DL 40　CD 40

1. Masa is thrilled to be watching the New York Yankees.　( T / F )
2. Ted thinks fall is the best time to watch a game.　( T / F )
3. Masa thinks baseball is better than soccer.　( T / F )
4. Ted is the same age as Masa's father.　( T / F )

**B** もう一度会話を聞いて、空所を埋めましょう。その後ペアになって、会話の練習をしましょう。

**Masa:** I can't believe I'm here tonight watching the New York Yankees! It's one of the (¹　　　) (²　　　　　) sports teams in the world.

**Ted:** And summer is the (³　　　　) time to watch a game, especially at night. It's (⁴　　　) and (⁵　　　) windy than during the day.

**Lucy:** What are the most (⁶　　　　) sports in Japan, Masa?

**Masa:** Baseball and soccer, I guess. But I think baseball is better. It's more (⁷　　　　).

**Lucy:** What about traditional sports like sumo?

**Masa:** For young people, sumo is less (⁸　　　　) than other sports. But old guys like my dad still like it. Ha ha ha!

**Ted:** How old is your father, Masa?

**Masa:** He's 45.

**Ted:** I'm 45.

**Masa:** Oops! …Ahhhh.

## Mission ! 1. 好みを伝えてみよう！

マサが自分は野球派だと述べている英文を探し、線を引きましょう。また、それを真似て次のセリフを言ってみましょう。

I _____ package tours _____ _____ than independent travel.

私はパッケージツアーの方が個人旅行よりもよいと思います。

Unit 10　Sports Talk

# Breaking Down the Grammar

● 比較級・最上級

**基本例文** Traveling by bus is **cheaper than** traveling by train.
バスで旅をするほうが電車で旅をするよりも安いです。

■ 2つのものを比べて「AはBより～だ」と言うときは、比較級を使います。

| 主語＋動詞 | 比較級 | than＋比較対象 | 意味 |
| --- | --- | --- | --- |
| My cousin is | young**er** | than me. | 私のいとこは私よりも若いです。 |
| A hard pillow is | **more** comfortable | than a soft pillow for me. | 私には柔らかい枕より硬い枕のほうが快適です。 |
| Cricket is | **less** popular | than soccer in Japan. | 日本ではクリケットはサッカーよりも人気がありません。 |

■ 3つ以上のものを比べて「Aが一番～だ」と言うときは、最上級を使います。

| 主語＋動詞 | 最上級 | 範囲を表す語句 | 意味 |
| --- | --- | --- | --- |
| This box is | **the** heav**iest** | of the three. | この箱は3つの中で一番重いです。 |
| Bob is | **the most** careful | driver in his family. | ボブは家族の中でもっとも注意深いドライバーです。 |
| I got | **the best** score | in my class. | 私はクラスで最高点を得ました。 |

■ そのほか、複数のものを比較する表現には以下のようなものがあります。

His latest movie is **as** interesting **as** his last one.
彼の最新映画は前作と同じくらい面白いです。

This is **one of the most** famous paintings in Japan.
これは日本でもっとも有名な絵の1つです。

■ 副詞も形容詞と同じように比較級・最上級を作ります。

The president spoke **more** slowly than usual.
大統領はいつもよりゆっくり話しました。

Tim runs **the** fast**est** of all the students in his class.
ティムはクラスの学生の中でもっとも速く走ります。

Do you have this coat in a larger size?

## Grammar Checking

**A** (　) 内から正しい選択肢を選び、文を完成させましょう。

1. Tokyo is ( **a.** big　**b.** more big　**c.** bigger ) than New York.
2. This morning, my train ran ( **a.** the most slowly　**b.** more slowly　**c.** very slowly ) than usual.
3. That camera is good, but this one is ( **a.** better　**b.** more better　**c.** better than ).
4. Yesterday was ( **a.** hottest　**b.** most hottest　**c.** the hottest ) day of the year.
5. Sandra works ( **a.** the hardly　**b.** the hard　**c.** the hardest ) of all the workers in her company.
6. What's ( **a.** the quickly　**b.** the quickest　**c.** the most quickly ) way to the station?
7. This café serves ( **a.** more　**b.** more than　**c.** the most ) delicious coffee in town!
8. Tom is not ( **a.** as good to　**b.** as best as　**c.** as good as ) top world-class players.

**B** [　] 内の形容詞や副詞を比較級または最上級にして、書き入れましょう。

1. Hokkaido is _____ area of Japan in winter.　[cold]
2. Canada is a little _____ than the United States.　[big]
3. Jennifer says _____ things sometimes.　[strange]
4. Danny is one of _____ people I know.　[friendly]
5. Susan works _____ than Alice.　[carefully]
6. What was _____ subject for you in high school?　[difficult]
7. Paul is a bad singer, but Harry is even _____.　[bad]
8. Of the three boys, Kenji can jump _____.　[far]

## Mission  2. 比較級と最上級を使ってみよう！

次の日本語を英語に直しましょう。

1. アメリカンフットボールは野球よりも危険です。　　　＊危険な dangerous

   _____

2. 図書館は大学の中で一番静かな場所です。

   _____

## Reading — Masa's Log

**A** マサのインターン日記「ニューヨークのスポーツチーム」を読み、表内の 1 〜 4 の空所に入るチーム名を選択肢から選びましょう。 CheckLink  DL 41  CD 41

### New York – A Sports Fan's Paradise

For sports fans, there's no better place to be than New York. It has eight teams in the four most popular sports leagues in North America: the Yankees and Mets in baseball, the Giants and Jets in football, the Knicks and Nets in basketball, and the Rangers and Islanders in hockey. There are two men's and one women's professional soccer teams, too. New York also hosts the U.S. Open tennis tournament and the New York City Marathon, the largest marathon in the world.

## Sports Teams in New York

| | |
|---|---|
| **Baseball (MLB)**  | • New York Yankees<br>• New York (¹    ) |
| **Football (NFL)**  | • New York (²    )<br>• New York Jets |
| **Basketball (NBA)**  | • New York (³    )<br>• Brooklyn Nets |
| **Hockey (NHL)**  | • New York Rangers<br>• New York (⁴    ) |

**a.** Giants  **b.** Islanders  **c.** Knicks  **d.** Mets

**B** 英文をもう一度読み、正しい選択肢を選びましょう。

1. New York has ( **a.** eight  **b.** eleven ) professional sports teams.
2. The U.S. Open is a ( **a.** tennis  **b.** soccer ) tournament.
3. New York has ( **a.** two  **b.** three ) professional soccer teams.

## Wrap-Up Writing

**A** さまざまなことがらに関するマサの価値観について、読んでみましょう。

**Masa's Opinion**
① IMPORTANT ✓love / money
② GOOD ✓a fun job with a low salary / a boring job with a high salary
③ INTERESTING living in the country / ✓living in the city
④ EASY SUBJECT ✓English / math / science
⑤ BAD SEASON spring / summer / fall / ✓winter

**B** **A** の情報を文にまとめてみましょう。①〜③は比較級の英文、④と⑤は最上級の英文にしてください。

① For Masa, _____ is more important than _____. ② A fun job with a low salary is _____ _____ a boring job with a high salary. ③ Living in the _____ is _____ _____ than living in the _____. ④ English is the _____ subject. ⑤ And winter is _____ _____ season.

**Mission** ❗ **3.** あなた自身について書いてみよう！

あなた自身について **A** の質問に答えた後、**A** と **B** を参考にして、あなたの価値観について書いてみましょう。

For me, _____ is more important _____
_____
_____
_____
_____

Unit 10　Sports Talk

# Unit 11 Tour Day

**Mission**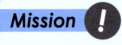
- 同僚に確認する
- 助動詞の使い方に慣れる
- 大学の規則について書く

## Getting Ready

**A** 英語の意味に合う日本語を a〜e から選びましょう。

CheckLink　DL 42　CD 42

1. shake hands　　　( )　　a. 高齢の乗客
2. elderly passenger　( )　　b. 確認する
3. make sure　　　　( )　　c. 名札
4. departure　　　　( )　　d. 握手をする
5. name tag　　　　( )　　e. 出発

**B** ツアーバスの前で話しているマサとパティのイラストを見ながら1〜4の英文を聞きましょう。イラストと合っていればT、異なっていればFを選びましょう。

CheckLink　DL 43　CD 43

1. T / F　　2. T / F　　3. T / F　　4. T / F

## Conversation

● *Lending a Helping Hand*

ツアー当日の朝。マサはパティから、添乗の仕事について指示を受けています。

**A** 会話を聞きましょう。1～4について、聞き取った内容と合っていればT、異なっていればFを選びましょう。

1. Patty asks Masa to greet the people outside the bus. ( T / F )
2. One passenger needs help to get on and off the bus. ( T / F )
3. Thirty-four people are taking the tour. ( T / F )
4. Masa doesn't have to wear his name tag in the bus. ( T / F )

**B** もう一度会話を聞いて、空所を埋めましょう。その後ペアになって、会話の練習をしましょう。

**Patty:** Masa, please greet the customers outside the bus.
**Masa:** OK. Should I shake hands with them?
**Patty:** No, you (¹           ) (²           ) to do that. But you (³           ) need to help the elderly passengers. Some of them (⁴           ) get on and off the bus by themselves.
**Masa:** Sure. I'll be happy to do that.
**Patty:** And (⁵           ) you make sure everyone is on the bus before departure? There will be 34 passengers.
**Masa:** Thirty-four. Got it.
**Patty:** Oh, and here's your name tag. You (⁶           ) wear it at all times. You (⁷           ) lose it.
**Masa:** All right. Umm, do I have (⁸           ) wear it to bed, too?
**Patty:** Very funny. Ha…ha.

### Mission ! 1. 相手に確認してみよう!

マサが接客の際にすべきことをパティにたずねている英文を探し、線を引きましょう。また、それを真似て次のセリフを言ってみましょう。

_____ I _____ him my business card first?
私が先に、彼に名刺を渡すべきですか。

## Breaking Down the Grammar　　●助動詞

　You **can** park your car in front of the shop.
あなたはお店の前に駐車することができます。

■ 助動詞には、動詞に意味をつけ加える役割があります。

| 助動詞 | 例文 |
|---|---|
| **can / could**<br>〜できる・できた | My father **can / could** cook well.<br>私の父は上手に料理することができます（できました）。 |
| **may / might**<br>〜かもしれない | We **may / might** arrive at the hotel late tonight.<br>私たちは今夜遅くにホテルに到着するかもしれません。 |
| **should**<br>〜すべき | You **should** buy tickets in advance.<br>あなたは前もってチケットを買うべきです。 |
| **must**<br>〜しなければならない | You **must** show your passport here.<br>あなたはここでパスポートを見せなければなりません。 |
| **have to**<br>〜しなければならない | We **have to** be home by 7:00.<br>私たちは7時までに帰宅しなければなりません。 |

［否定文］

You **must not** enter this building with your shoes on.
靴を履いてこの建物に入ってはいけません。

You **don't have to** take off your hat in this room.
あなたはこの部屋では帽子を脱ぐ必要はありません。

［疑問文］

**Should** I leave a tip on the table?　テーブルにチップを置いていくべきですか。

**Do** we **have to** memorize all the words on the list?
このリストにある単語をすべて覚えなければなりませんか。

■ 助動詞は疑問文で、依頼や許可の意味も表します。

**Can** you pass me the milk, please?
ミルクを取ってくれませんか。

**May** I ask you questions by email?
メールで質問してもよいですか。

# Grammar Checking

**A** ( ) 内から正しい選択肢を選び、文を完成させましょう。　CheckLink

1. Sandra can ( **a.** sing   **b.** to sing   **c.** singing ) beautifully.
2. You look tired. You ( **a.** couldn't   **b.** shouldn't   **c.** might not ) work so hard.
3. You ( **a.** may   **b.** must   **c.** can ) be careful here. It's dangerous.
4. I ( **a.** had to   **b.** must   **c.** should ) work late last night.
5. Take a sweater. You ( **a.** have to   **b.** might   **c.** should ) need it later.
6. It was dark. I ( **a.** could   **b.** can't   **c.** couldn't ) see anything.
7. Tom ( **a.** may not   **b.** can't   **c.** must not ) go to the party. He's not sure.
8. We ( **a.** have to   **b.** don't have to   **c.** didn't have to ) wait long. The bus came soon.

**B** 以下の英文には誤りが含まれています。例にならって誤りを含む箇所に線を引き、英文全体を正しく書き直しましょう。

1. John can ~~swims~~ very well.　→　_John can swim very well._
2. She have to get up early every day.
   → _____
3. Last night, I must attend a meeting.
   → _____
4. Today is a national holiday, so we don't must work.
   → _____
5. I might late for class tomorrow.
   → _____

## Mission  2. 助動詞を使って書いてみよう！

次の日本語を英語に直しましょう。

1. アサミは英語でとてもよいプレゼンをすることができます。
　　　　　　　　　　　　　　　　　　　＊プレゼンをする　make presentations

_____

2. イングランドでは、左側運転をしなければなりません。　　＊左側で　on the left

_____

Unit 11　Tour Day

# Reading

*Masa's Log*

**A** マサのインターン日記「アメリカのチップ制度」を読み、イラスト1～4のサービスのうち、チップが必要なものには○を、不要なものには×を入れましょう。

## Tipping

In the United States, there is a tipping custom for various services. At a restaurant, you should leave a 15% to 20% tip for the waiter. You should tip taxi drivers, hairdressers and pizza delivery persons 15% to 20%, too. And you shouldn't forget to leave a tip for the hotel maid – usually $2 to $4 per night. You don't usually have to tip hotel doormen, front desk clerks, or fast food restaurant workers.

1. (　　)

2. (　　)

3. (　　)

4. (　　)

**B** 英文をもう一度読み、正しい選択肢を選びましょう。

1. A tip for a meal that costs $20 should be ( **a.** $2-$3　**b.** $3-$4 ).
2. It is common to tip a ( **a.** hairdresser　**b.** front desk clerk ).
3. You should leave ( **a.** $1　**b.** a few dollars ) per night for the hotel maid.

## Wrap-Up Writing

**A** プリーズトラベル社の社内ルールを読んでみましょう。

**Must / Mustn't**
○ wear business clothes when meeting customers
× smoke or eat in front of customers

**Should / Shouldn't**
○ answer the phone within two rings
× stay at the office after 8:00 p.m.

**Can / Can't**
○ join any one-day tour at half price
× take time off during busy seasons

**Notes:** within two rings「2コール以内で」 take time off「休暇を取る」

**B** **A** の情報を文にまとめてみましょう。（　　）には助動詞を入れてください。

You (　　　　) wear business clothes when meeting customers. You (　　　　) smoke or eat in front of _____. You (　　　　) answer the phone within two rings. You shouldn't _____ at the office after 8:00 p.m. You can _____ any one-day tour at half price. You (　　　　) take time _____ during busy seasons.

### Mission  3. あなた自身について書いてみよう！

**A** と **B** を参考にして、あなたの大学でのルールについて書いてみましょう。must / mustn't と can / can't の4つを使ってください。

1. We must _____
2. We mustn't _____
3. We can _____
4. We can't _____

**Hints**　be absent more than 3 times「3回以上欠席する」　borrow the textbook from a friend「友だちに教科書を借りる」　take math classes「数学を受講する」　eat in the library「図書館で食べる」　write a report each semester「毎学期レポートを書く」　sleep during class「授業中居眠りをする」

# Unit 12 Party Time!

**Mission**
- 喜びを伝える
- 現在完了形を理解する
- 最近したことについて書く

## Getting Ready

**A** 英語の意味に合う日本語をa〜eから選びましょう。

CheckLink　DL 46　CD 46

1. lover　　　　　（　）　　a. 〜といえば
2. speaking of　（　）　　b. 〜を除いて
3. text　　　　　（　）　　c. 事故、トラブル
4. accident　　 （　）　　d. 愛好家
5. except　　　 （　）　　e. メッセージを送る

**B** オフィスでのポットラック・パーティーのイラストを見ながら1〜4の英文を聞きましょう。イラストと合っていればT、異なっていればFを選びましょう。

CheckLink　DL 47　CD 47

1. T / F　　2. T / F　　3. T / F　　4. T / F

## Conversation

● *Please Travel Potluck Party*

今夜は会社のポットラック・パーティー。パティとルーシーが話をしています。

**A** 会話を聞きましょう。1〜4について、聞き取った内容と合っていればT、異なっていればFを選びましょう。

CheckLink　DL 48　CD 48

1. This is Lucy's first time to go to a potluck party. ( T / F )
2. Lucy's bagels are popular. ( T / F )
3. Masa called and texted Patty. ( T / F )
4. Masa was working late at the office. ( T / F )

**B** もう一度会話を聞いて、空所を埋めましょう。その後ペアになって、会話の練習をしましょう。

**Lucy:** I've never ($^1$　　　) to a potluck party before, Patty.
**Patty:** I'm glad you could come. Everyone *loves* your bagels!
**Lucy:** Everyone except Masa. Ha ha ha!
**Patty:** Yeah, Masa's not a bagel lover.
**Lucy:** Speaking of Masa, have you ($^2$　　　) him?
**Patty:** Actually, no. And he ($^3$　　　) called or ($^4$　　　) me. I hope he ($^5$　　　) ($^6$　　　) an accident.
**Masa:** Hi! Sorry I'm late!
**Patty:** Masa! Hi. Lucy and I were just talking about you. Where ($^7$　　　) you been?
**Masa:** ($^8$　　　) been busy in the kitchen. See?
**Patty:** Oh, it's a watermelon!
**Masa:** It's not just a watermelon. …Ta-da!

### Mission ❗ 1. 喜びを相手に伝えてみよう！

パティがルーシーを歓迎している英文を探し、線を引きましょう。また、それを真似て次のセリフを言ってみましょう。

＿＿＿＿＿ ＿＿＿＿＿ you joined our ＿＿＿＿＿.
あなたが入社してくれて嬉しいです。

# Breaking Down the Grammar

● 現在完了形

My boyfriend **has gone** to Canada. I **haven't seen** him for three months.

私のボーイフレンドはカナダに行ってしまいました。3 か月間会っていません。

■ 現在完了形は、今までに経験したこと（経験）や、ずっと続けていること（継続）、やり終えたこと（完了）などについて述べるときに使います。

|  | 主語 | have＋過去分詞 | その他の情報 | 意味 |
|---|---|---|---|---|
| 経験 | I | **have tried** | skydiving once. | 私は一度スカイダイビングをしたことがあります。 |
| 継続 | We | **have known** | each other since kindergarten. | 私たちは幼稚園の頃から知り合いです。 |
|  | Lisa | **has had** | her pet rabbit for two years. | リサはペットのうさぎを 2 年間飼っています。 |
| 完了 | Chris | **has** already **finished** | packing for his trip. | クリスはすでに旅支度を終えました。 |

▶ once「一度」や many times「何度も」など回数を表す語句は経験、since「～以来」や for「～の間」は継続、already「すでに」は完了の文で用いられることが多いです。

[否定文]

I **haven't** [**have not**] read this book yet. 私はまだこの本を読んでいません。

Richard **has never tried** sushi. リチャードは一度も寿司を食べたことがありません。

[疑問文]

**Have** you ever **traveled** alone? あなたはこれまでに一人旅をしたことがありますか。

**Has** Jack **finished** his homework yet? —No, not yet.
ジャックはもう宿題をやり終えましたか。—いいえ、まだです。

How long **have** you **worked** for this company? —For ten years.
あなたはどれくらい長くこの会社に勤めていますか。—10 年です。

## Grammar Checking

**A** (　) 内から正しい選択肢を選び、文を完成させましょう。

1. Donna and Andy have ( **a.** go   **b.** gone   **c.** went ) to England.
2. I haven't seen Tim ( **a.** for   **b.** on   **c.** since ) last week.
3. We've already ( **a.** ate   **b.** eaten   **c.** eat ) dinner.
4. Soccer practice hasn't finished ( **a.** already   **b.** before   **c.** yet ).
5. ( **a.** Did   **b.** Has   **c.** Have ) everyone done their homework?
6. I ( **a.** have   **b.** have ever   **c.** haven't never ) been here before.
7. Oh, no! ( **a.** I've lost my key   **b.** I've my key lost   **c.** My key has lost ).
8. How ( **a.** long you have known   **b.** have you long known   **c.** long have you known ) Frank?

**B** 空所に適当な動詞を選択肢から選び、現在完了形にして書き入れましょう。

|  arrive   |   eat   |   have   |   live   |   meet   |   study   |
| --- | --- | --- | --- | --- | --- |

1. **A:** Are you all right, Kim?   **B:** No, I _____ _____ a headache all day.
2. **A:** _____ you _____ for your test?   **B:** No, not yet.
3. **A:** Is Greg here?   **B:** Yes, he _____ just _____.
4. **A:** How long _____ you _____ in Tokyo, Joe?   **B:** For about two years.
5. **A:** _____ you ever _____ octopus?   **B:** No, I don't like seafood.
6. **A:** Helen, this is Ryota.   **B:** Yes, we _____ already _____.

## Mission  2. 現在完了形を使ってみよう！

次の日本語を英語に直しましょう。

1. 私はまだ航空券を買っていません。　　　　　　　　＊航空券 airplane ticket

2. あなたはこれまで有名人に会ったことがありますか。　　　＊有名人 famous person

# Reading

*Masa's Log*

**A** マサのインターン日記を読み、写真a〜dを紹介されている順に並べ替えましょう。

### Things I Haven't Done — Yet

I've already done many fun things in New York. Here's a list of things I haven't done yet. First, I want to see a Broadway musical. In fact, I've already bought my ticket ($99 ☹). Second, I want to see New York from the top of the Empire State Building ($54 ☹). Visiting MoMA is third on my list. It normally costs $14 (☺), but I've decided to go on Friday between 4 p.m. and 8 p.m. It's free! ☺ Finally, I want to see Grand Central Terminal. It's free, too! ☺

***Note:*** MoMA (Museum of Modern Art)「ニューヨーク近代美術館」

¹(　　) ➡ ²(　　) ➡ ³(　　) ➡ ⁴(　　)

**B** 英文をもう一度読み、正しい選択肢を選びましょう。

1. Masa has bought a ticket to a Broadway ( **a.** concert  **b.** musical ).
2. Masa wants to go up the ( **a.** Statue of Liberty  **b.** Empire State Building ).
3. MoMA is free on Fridays ( **a.** after 8:00  **b.** from 4:00 to 8:00 ).

## Wrap-Up Writing

**A** 最近マサがしたこととしていないことについて、読んでみましょう。

| | |
|---|---|
| ○ have a haircut | ○ use an ATM |
| × play a video game | × clean your room |
| ○ go out for dinner | ○ buy some new clothes |
| × read a novel | × see a movie |

*Note:* novel「小説」

**B** **A** の情報を文にまとめてみましょう。動詞は現在完了形を使ってください。

Recently, Masa has _____ a haircut, _____ an ATM, _____ out for dinner and bought some new _____. He hasn't _____ a video game, _____ his room, read a _____ or _____ a movie.

### Mission ! 3. あなた自身について書いてみよう！

**A** と **B** を参考にして、あなたが最近したこととしていないことを3つずつ書いてみましょう。

Recently, I have _____
_____
_____
_____

**Hints**
play a sport「スポーツをする」　exercise「エクササイズをする」　have fresh fruit「果物を食べる」
write a report「レポートを書く」　go to the doctor/dentist「医者／歯医者に行く」
go to the zoo/a karaoke box「動物園／カラオケに行く」
see my high school friends「高校時代の友人に会う」

Unit 12　Party Time!

# Unit 13 Office Meeting

- 滞在先の感想をたずねる
- 関係詞を理解する
- 尊敬する人物について書く

## Getting Ready

**A** 英語の意味に合う日本語を a〜e から選びましょう。

1. take part       (　)     a. 理由
2. assist          (　)     b. かつら
3. reason          (　)     c. 予備の
4. wig             (　)     d. 助ける
5. spare           (　)     e. 参加する

**B** 社内会議に出席している社員たちのイラストを見ながら1〜4の英文を聞きましょう。イラストと合っていればT、異なっていればFを選びましょう。

1. T / F    2. T / F    3. T / F    4. T / F

## Conversation  ● A Few Problems

パティとマサは、先日添乗した『ナイアガラの滝ツアー』の社内報告をしています。

**A** 会話を聞きましょう。1〜4について、聞き取った内容と合っていればT、異なっていればFを選びましょう。

1. Forty-three people took the tour. ( T / F )
2. Everyone could see Niagara Falls from their hotel room. ( T / F )
3. A man lost his glasses in the river. ( T / F )
4. Masa got on the wrong bus. ( T / F )

**B** もう一度会話を聞いて、空所を埋めましょう。その後ペアになって、会話の練習をしましょう。

**Ted:** How was the Niagara Falls tour (¹_____) you conducted, Patty?

**Patty:** Good. There were 34 people (²_____) took part, and Masa assisted me.

**Ted:** Masa, what did you think of the hotel where you stayed?

**Masa:** Fantastic! All of the rooms had great views of the falls. That's the main reason (³_____) everyone liked it.

**Ted:** Any problems?

**Patty:** Well, there was one man (⁴_____) dropped his cellphone in the river.

**Masa:** And a lady (⁵_____) wig blew into Niagara Falls during the boat ride. Luckily, she had a spare wig (⁶_____) she could wear.

**Patty:** And then there was the guy (⁷_____) got on a bus (⁸_____) was full of cheerleaders.

**Masa:** Oh, yeah, that was me. …Lucky me! Ha ha ha!

### Mission ! 1. 相手に感想をたずねてみよう！

テッドがマサにホテルの感想をたずねている英文を探し、線を引きましょう。また、それを真似て次のセリフを言ってみましょう。

What did you _____ _____ the food that you _____ at the restaurant?
そのレストランで食べた食べ物についてあなたはどう思いましたか。

## Breaking Down the Grammar　　●関係詞

 The man **who** is wearing the navy suit is my boss.
紺色のスーツを着ている男性は私の上司です。

■「私が昨日会った人」のように名詞に説明を加える場合、関係詞を使います。説明を加えたい名詞が人の場合は who [that] を、それ以外の場合は that [which] を使います。

| 名詞 | 名詞についての説明 | 意味 |
| --- | --- | --- |
| the girl | **who** is singing on the stage | 舞台の上で歌っている女の子 |
| the book | **that** [**which**] I bought yesterday | 私が昨日買った本 |

[例] Do you remember the girl **who** we met during our trip to Osaka?
あなたは大阪旅行で会った女の子を覚えていますか。

The book **that** [**which**] I bought yesterday was interesting.
私が昨日買った本は面白かったです。

I met a woman **whose** grandfather used to live in Japan.
私は、祖父がかつて日本に住んでいたという女性に会いました。

■関係詞の why, where, when は「理由」「場所」「時」を表す名詞に説明を加えます。

| 名詞 | 名詞についての説明 | 意味 |
| --- | --- | --- |
| the reason | **why** Mary is angry | メアリーが怒っている理由 |
| the place | **where** we had dinner together | 一緒に夕食を食べた場所 |
| the time | **when** I was in Tokyo | 私が東京にいた時 |

[例] Nobody knew the reason **why** Mary was angry.
誰もメアリーが怒っている理由を知りませんでした。

That was the day **when** I started my internship.
それは私がインターンを始めた日でした。

# Grammar Checking

**A** (　　) 内から正しい選択肢を選び、文を完成させましょう。　　CheckLink

1. The man ( **a.** who　**b.** who's　**c.** whose ) called didn't give his name.
2. The book ( **a.** that　**b.** what　**c.** that's ) I'm reading is very interesting.
3. I have a friend ( **a.** who　**b.** who's　**c.** whose ) a professional dancer.
4. The team ( **a.** that　**b.** where　**c.** who ) won the game was very strong.
5. The people ( **a.** who　**b.** which　**c.** whose ) work there are all very nice.
6. Sunday is the day ( **a.** where　**b.** which　**c.** when ) I do my laundry.
7. Did you like the hotel ( **a.** that　**b.** where　**c.** which ) you stayed?
8. That's the lady ( **a.** that　**b.** which　**c.** whose ) dog bit me.

**B** 空所に適切な関係詞を入れて、英文を完成させましょう。

1. Do you know anyone ＿＿＿＿ can speak French?
2. Sally always wears clothes ＿＿＿＿ are bright and colorful.
3. The food at the restaurant ＿＿＿＿ we ate was excellent!
4. Bruce found a shop ＿＿＿＿ sells clothes from the 1950s.
5. My apartment was small and very old. That's the reason ＿＿＿＿ I moved.
6. I have a friend ＿＿＿＿ parents have a small hotel near the sea.
7. Golden Week is a time ＿＿＿＿ many people take trips.
8. A true friend is someone ＿＿＿＿ you can always depend on.

## Mission　2. 関係詞を使って書いてみよう！

次の日本語を英語に直しましょう。

1. サングラスをかけている女性は私の上司です。

2. 私が受講しているダンスのレッスンはとても楽しいです。

# Reading

● *Masa's Log*

**A** マサのインターン日記を読み、イラストa～dを述べられている順に並べ替えましょう。

CheckLink　DL 53　CD 53

## Company Meetings

I've attended half a dozen meetings that Please Travel has held. Like in Japan, everyone who attends meetings arrives on time. Before talking business, we always chat for a few minutes with the person who is sitting next to us. Here, people are not afraid to disagree with the boss. This is rare in Japan, I think. My father always says, "I never argue with the boss." Our meetings are always 45 minutes long. This is also rare in Japan. My father says he never knows when the meetings will end at the company where he works.

*Notes:* half a dozen「12の半分」 disagree「反対する」 argue「口論する」

¹(　　) ➡ ²(　　) ➡ ³(　　) ➡ ⁴(　　)

**B** 英文をもう一度読み、正しい選択肢を選びましょう。　CheckLink

1. Masa has attended ( **a.** six　**b.** twelve ) Please Travel meetings.
2. Masa's father ( **a.** never disagrees　**b.** always argues ) with his boss.
3. Masa's father's meetings ( **a.** always start a few minutes late　**b.** have no fixed ending time ).

## Wrap-Up Writing

**A** マサが尊敬する人物についての情報を読んでみましょう。

> **Who is someone you respect?** Patty Anderson
> **What is your relation to this person?** co-worker at Please Travel
> **Why do you respect this person?**
> - hard-working, diligent
> - listens to everyone's opinions
> - gives me a lot of information and advice

*Note:* relation「関係」

**B** **A** の情報を文にまとめてみましょう。（　　）には関係詞を入れてください。

Patty Anderson is a person (　　　　) Masa respects. She is Masa's _____ at Please Travel. There are several reasons (　　　　) Masa respects her. First, she is hard-working and _____. Second, she _____ to everyone's opinions. Finally, she gives him a lot of _____ and advice.

### Mission ! 3. あなた自身について書いてみよう！

**A** と **B** を参考にして、あなたが尊敬する人物について書いてみましょう。

_____ is a person _____ I respect. _____ is my _____. There are several reasons _____

First, _____

Second, _____

Finally, _____

**Hints** my high school teacher「高校時代の先生」　a senior in my club「クラブの先輩」　smart「賢い」　independent「独立心のある」　a good leader「よいリーダー」　treat everyone fairly「みんなを公平に扱う」　make everyone around him/her feel relaxed「周りのみんなを心地よくさせる」

# Unit 14 A Bit of History

**Mission**
- 観光名所を案内する
- 受動態を理解する
- 通っている大学について書く

## Getting Ready

**A** 英語の意味に合う日本語を a〜e から選びましょう。

CheckLink　DL 54　CD 54

1. neighborhood　(　)　　a. 設立する
2. must-see　　　(　)　　b. 単に
3. row house　　 (　)　　c. 地区
4. found　　　　 (　)　　d. 長屋建て住宅
5. simply　　　　(　)　　e. 見るべきもの

**B** ニューヨークのグリニッジ・ビレッジのイラストを見ながら 1〜4 の英文を聞きましょう。イラストと合っていれば T、異なっていれば F を選びましょう。

CheckLink　DL 55　CD 55

1. T / F　　2. T / F　　3. T / F　　4. T / F

## Conversation
● In "the Village"

マサはプリーズトラベル社の観光案内ツアーに参加してみることにしました。

**A** 会話を聞きましょう。1～4について、聞き取った内容と合っていればT、異なっていればFを選びましょう。

1. A few guidebooks recommend visiting Greenwich Village. ( T / F )
2. Greenwich Village is a historical area of New York. ( T / F )
3. The row houses are more than 100 years old. ( T / F )
4. The main campus of NYU opened in 1931. ( T / F )

**B** もう一度会話を聞いて、空所を埋めましょう。その後ペアになって、会話の練習をしましょう。

**Masa:** This is an interesting neighborhood. What's it (¹_____)?
**Guide:** Greenwich Village, but it's known to New Yorkers as simply "the Village." It's (²_____) in all the guidebooks as a must-see in New York.
**Masa:** It looks like a very old area.
**Guide:** It is. These row houses (³_____) built in the 1800s. NYU's main campus (⁴_____) also (⁵_____) here. It was (⁶_____) in 1831. And Washington Square Park is (⁷_____) to be one of New York's best parks.
**Masa:** I guess a lot of artists and musicians are (⁸_____) here. It's so cool!
**Guide:** Yeah! And speaking of cool, Masa, you look very cool today.
**Masa:** Well, we *are* going to a jazz club.
**Guide:** OK, everyone, are you ready for some great jazz?

*Note:* NYU「ニューヨーク大学」

### Mission  1. 観光名所を案内してみよう！

ガイドさんがグリニッジ・ビレッジの愛称について述べている英文を探し、線を引きましょう。また、それを真似て次のセリフを言ってみましょう。

Paris _____ _____ _____ the "City of Love."
パリは「愛の街」として知られています。

# Breaking Down the Grammar

● 受動態

 **Japan is visited** by millions of tourists every year.
日本は毎年何百万人もの観光客に訪問されています。

■ 人やものが「～される／された」という意味を表す場合、受動態を使います。受動態の文を作るときは、主語の後に be 動詞＋過去分詞を続けます。

| 主語 | be動詞＋過去分詞 | その他の情報 | 意味 |
|---|---|---|---|
| These roses | **were grown** | by my mother. | これらのバラは私の母によって育てられました。 |
| This temple | **was built** | in Kyoto in 1397. | この寺は1397年に京都に建てられました。 |
| The airline | **is known** | for its good service. | その航空会社はサービスのよさで知られています。 |
| This shopping bag | **is made** | of paper. | この買い物袋は紙で作られています。 |

▶「～によって」と動作の主体となる人を表すときには、by ~ をつけます。
▶ by 以下のない受動態や、そのほかの前置詞（for, as, of など）が来るものもあります。

［否定文］

French **isn't taught** at this school. この学校ではフランス語は教えられていません。

Comic books **aren't sold** at this bookstore. この本屋では漫画は売られていません。

［疑問文］

**Are** these shoes **made** in Italy?
この靴はイタリア製ですか。

**Were** these avocados **imported** from Mexico?
これらのアボカドはメキシコから輸入されましたか。

When **was** your company **founded**?
御社はいつ設立されましたか。

Sorry, no pets are allowed.

## Grammar Checking

**A** (　　) 内から正しい選択肢を選び、文を完成させましょう。　　CheckLink

1. This table ( **a.** has　**b.** is　**c.** does ) made of wood.
2. The trash ( **a.** is collected　**b.** is collecting　**c.** collects ) every Monday.
3. These pictures ( **a.** are taken　**b.** were taking　**c.** were taken ) last year.
4. Where ( **a.** are you　**b.** you were　**c.** were you ) born?
5. When ( **a.** was the party held　**b.** was held the party　**c.** the party was held )?
6. Was ( **a.** sung this song　**b.** this song was sung　**c.** this song sung ) by Michael?
7. Luckily, no one ( **a.** was　**b.** were　**c.** wasn't ) hurt in the accident.
8. How ( **a.** is written your name　**b.** is your name written　**c.** your name is written )?

**B** (　　) 内の語句を並べ替えて、日本語に合う文を作りましょう。

1. ( cleaned / our / every / is / classroom )　私たちの教室は毎週土曜に清掃されます。
   _____ Saturday.

2. ( in / was / England / built / ship / this )　この船はイギリス製です。
   _____.

3. ( my / by / pictures / drawn / friend / these / were )
   これらの絵は私の友人によって描かれました。
   _____.

4. ( party / to / people / were / many / invited / the )
   多くの人がパーティーに招待されたのですか。
   _____?

## Mission　2. 受動態を使ってみよう！

次の日本語を英語に直しましょう。

1. これらのじゃがいもは北海道で育てられました。
   _____

2. この駅は毎日約100万人の人々によって利用されています。　　＊100万 one million
   _____

# Reading

*Masa's Log*

**A** マサのインターン日記を読み、表内の空所1～4に当てはまる数字を選択肢から選びましょう。

CheckLink　DL 57　CD 57

## The Statue of Liberty

The world famous Statue of Liberty is on Liberty Island in New York Harbor. It was given to the United States by France in 1886. The plan was to give the statue to America on July 4, 1876 – its 100th birthday. However, it wasn't completed until 10 years later. It is 93 meters from the ground to the top of the torch. The statue itself is 46 meters tall and weighs about 200,000 kg. It is visited by about 4 million people a year.

### Statue of Liberty Facts

| | | |
|---|---|---|
| Height from the ground | ( $^1$     ) meters | |
| Height of the statue only | ( $^2$     ) meters | |
| Weight of the statue | ( $^3$     ) kilograms | |
| Number of visitors each year | ( $^4$     ) people | |

a. 46　b. 93　c. 100　d. 200,000　e. 400,000　f. 4,000,000

**B** 英文をもう一度読み、正しい選択肢を選びましょう。　CheckLink

1. The Statue of Liberty is on ( **a.** Liberty Island　**b.** Staten Island ).
2. The statue was built by the ( **a.** Americans　**b.** French ).
3. The United States became a country in ( **a.** 1776　**b.** 1876 ).

## Wrap-Up Writing

**A** マサが通う大学の情報を読んでみましょう。

| | |
|---:|:---|
| Name of college or university: | Sakuhana University |
| Month and year of acceptance: | February 2017 |
| Location: | Tokyo, Japan |
| Nearest train or subway station: | Hana Station |
| Number of students attending: | about 4,000 |

**Note:** acceptance「合格、(入学の) 受け入れ」

**B** **A** の情報を文にまとめてみましょう。

Masa goes to Sakuhana _____. He _____ accepted into the university in _____ 2017. The university is _____ in Tokyo, Japan. The _____ subway station is called Hana Station. The university _____ attended by about 4,000 _____.

### Mission ! 3. あなた自身について書いてみよう！

**A** と **B** を参考にして、あなたの通う大学について書いてみましょう。

I go to _____

_____

_____

_____

_____

# Unit 15 Farewell, Masa and Lucy

**Mission**
- お別れの言葉を述べる
- 接続詞の使い方に慣れる
- 普段の習慣について書く

## Getting Ready

**A** 英語の意味に合う日本語を a〜e から選びましょう。

CheckLink  DL 58  CD 58

1. unfortunately ( )        a. おもてなし
2. miss ( )                  b. 必ず〜する
3. be sure to ( )            c. 残念ながら
4. experience ( )            d. 寂しく思う
5. hospitality ( )           e. 経験

**B** カフェのテラス席に集うマサたちのイラストを見ながら 1〜4 の英文を聞きましょう。イラストと合っていれば T、異なっていれば F を選びましょう。

CheckLink  DL 59  CD 59

1. T / F    2. T / F    3. T / F    4. T / F

## Conversation

● Last Day

午前の業務を終えた社員たち。テッドの誘いでカフェにやって来ました。

**A** 会話を聞きましょう。1〜4について、聞き取った内容と合っていればT、異なっていればFを選びましょう。

CheckLink　DL 60　CD 60

1. Ted is sad because Masa's and Lucy's internship has ended. ( T / F )
2. Lucy's internship lasted one month. ( T / F )
3. Masa thanks everyone for visiting him in the hospital. ( T / F )
4. Masa will think of hot dogs when he wears his T-shirt in Japan. ( T / F )

**B** もう一度会話を聞いて、空所を埋めましょう。その後ペアになって、会話の練習をしましょう。

**Ted:** We're sad (¹　　　　), unfortunately, today was your last day. We'll all miss you (²　　　　) you return to your countries. Be sure to visit us (³　　　　) you're ever in New York again.

**Lucy:** Thanks, Ted. (⁴　　　　　) my internship was only for a month, it was a great experience.

**Masa:** Yes, thank you. I learned a lot (⁵　　　　) I was here. I'll never forget your kindness and hospitality.

**Patty:** (⁶　　　　　) you leave, we have a small gift for you. Lucy, this special bagel T-shirt is for you.

**Lucy:** It's so cute! Thank you.

**Patty:** And Masa, (⁷　　　　) you like hot dogs so much, we made a special hot dog T-shirt for you.

**Masa:** Thanks! I'll think of all of you (⁸　　　　) I wear it in Japan.

### Mission ❗ 1. お別れの言葉を言ってみよう！

マサが親切にしてもらったことを感謝している英文を探し、線を引きましょう。また、それを真似て次のセリフを言ってみましょう。

　　I'll _____ _____ _____ support and encouragement.
　　あなたの応援と励ましを私は決して忘れません。

Unit 15　Farewell, Masa and Lucy

## Breaking Down the Grammar　　●接続詞

**Please turn off the light before you leave the room.**
あなたが部屋を出る前に、電気を消してください。

■接続詞は、2つ以上の語句や文をつなげる働きをします。

| 接続詞 | 例文 |
|---|---|
| after ～の後に<br>before ～の前に | Call me after/before you arrive at the station.<br>駅到着後に／前に、私に電話してください。 |
| while<br>～の間に | While Lisa was cooking, I did the laundry.<br>リサが料理をしている間、私は洗濯をしました。 |
| when<br>～するとき | I was taking a bath when you called me.<br>あなたが電話してきたとき、私はお風呂に入っていました。 |
| until<br>～まで | We practiced until it got dark.<br>私たちは暗くなるまで練習しました。 |
| if<br>もし | If you study hard, you will pass the exam.<br>もし一生懸命勉強すれば、あなたは試験に合格するでしょう。 |
| because /<br>since<br>～なので | We couldn't buy a drink because the cafeteria was closed.<br>カフェテリアが閉まっていたので、私たちは飲み物を買えませんでした。<br>Since the weather is bad, we should stay home.<br>天気が悪いので、私たちは家にいるべきです。<br>▶話し手と聞き手の両方にとって明らかな理由を述べるときは since が好まれます。 |
| although<br>～だけれども | Although it was raining, I went for a walk.<br>雨が降っていたけれど、私は散歩に行きました。 |
| unless<br>～でない限り | You can't get the job unless you have experience.<br>経験がない限り、あなたはその仕事を得ることはできません。 |

Did you close the door before we left?

# Grammar Checking

**A** ( ) 内から正しい選択肢を選び、文を完成させましょう。

1. We didn't go out ( **a.** although   **b.** because   **c.** until ) it was raining.
2. ( **a.** After   **b.** If   **c.** While ) Dan graduated from college, he began working.
3. I'll call you ( **a.** since   **b.** until   **c.** when ) I arrive at the station.
4. ( **a.** Although   **b.** Because   **c.** Since ) Tom studied hard, he failed the test.
5. Let's wait here ( **a.** if   **b.** since   **c.** until ) Walter comes.
6. I'll wash the dishes ( **a.** although   **b.** because   **c.** if ) you dry them.
7. I saw Justin ( **a.** unless   **b.** until   **c.** while ) I was shopping.
8. Sorry, you can't enter ( **a.** if   **b.** when   **c.** unless ) you have a ticket.

**B** 1〜6の英文に続く適切な選択肢をa〜fから選びましょう。

1. Ai always texts her boyfriend   [   ]   **a.** while I was taking a bath.
2. We played tennis   [   ]   **b.** unless you have a good reason.
3. Dave failed the class   [   ]   **c.** if you can't do it yourself.
4. The phone rang   [   ]   **d.** before she goes to bed.
5. I'll help you   [   ]   **e.** because he never studied.
6. You can't leave early   [   ]   **f.** until it got dark.

**Mission** 2. 接続詞を使って書いてみよう！

次の日本語を英語に直しましょう。

1. あなたが今日帰る前に、あなたに話す必要があります。

　

2. 私はたくさんのすべき仕事があるので、今夜は遅くまで起きているでしょう。
   　　　　　　　　　　　　　　　　＊遅くまで起きている stay up late

## Reading

● *Masa's Log*

**A** マサのインターン日記を読み、イラストa〜dを述べられている順に並べ替えましょう。

CheckLink　DL 61　CD 61

### Shaking Hands, Hugging and Kissing

Since I came to New York, I've noticed that people shake hands a lot. Of course, it's common in business, but when I go out, I often see friends shaking hands, too. Girls often hug each other, and girls and guys often hug. It's not unusual to see old couples holding hands while they are walking. It all looks very natural to me. Because today was my last day, Ted shook my hand, and Lucy and Patty both kissed me. I'm still in heaven!

¹(　　) ➡ ²(　　) ➡ ³(　　) ➡ ⁴(　　)

**B** 英文をもう一度読み、正しい選択肢を選びましょう。

CheckLink

1. Masa thinks hugging and holding hands in public is ( **a.** natural　**b.** romantic ).
2. Ted ( **a.** hugged Masa　**b.** shook Masa's hand ).
3. Masa is happy because he ( **a.** received a gift　**b.** was kissed ).

## Wrap-Up Writing

**A** マサが普段の習慣について答えたアンケートを読んでみましょう。

### What do you usually do …

Q1: … after you get dressed in the morning?　　eat breakfast

Q2: … while you are riding the train?　　read the newspaper

Q3: … before you go to bed?　　have a cup of tea

Q4: … if you can't sleep at night?　　do some exercise

**B** **A**の情報を文にまとめてみましょう。(　　)には接続詞を入れてください。

Masa usually eats breakfast (　　　　) he gets _____ in the morning. While he is riding the train, he usually _____ the newspaper. (　　　　) he goes to bed, he usually has a _____ of tea. (　　　　) he can't sleep at night, he usually _____ some exercise.

**Mission❗ 3.** あなた自身について書いてみよう！

あなた自身について**A**の質問に答えた後、**B**を参考にしてあなたの普段の習慣について書いてみましょう。

I usually _____

While I _____

Before I _____

If _____

**Hints**: wash my face「顔を洗う」　put on my make-up「メイクをする」　read a book「本を読む」　use my cellphone「携帯電話を使う」　prepare for the next day「翌日の準備をする」　check my mail「メールチェックをする」　drink hot milk「ホットミルクを飲む」　play with my cat「ネコと遊ぶ」

Unit 15　Farewell, Masa and Lucy

# 会話表現 & 基本例文一覧

*Mission! 1* で学習した会話表現と、Breaking Down the Grammar の基本例文の一覧です。空所を埋めてみましょう。

### Unit 1　[お礼を伝える／現在形]

| | |
|---|---|
| ☐ ニューヨークに来てくれてありがとう。 | _____ for _____ to New York. |
| ☐ 私は日本出身です。ニューヨークで働いています。 | I _____ from Japan. I _____ in New York. |

### Unit 2　[感想を述べる／代名詞]

| | |
|---|---|
| ☐ 正直なところ、タイ料理はあまり好きではありません。 | To ____ _____, I don't really _____ Thai food. |
| ☐ これらのクッキーはおいしそうです。私はこれらを食べてみたいです。 | These cookies look delicious. I want to try _____ . |

### Unit 3　[勤務時間についてたずねる／前置詞]

| | |
|---|---|
| ☐ 勤務時間は 8:30 から 4:30 までですか。 | Are office _____ _____ 8:30 _____ 4:30? |
| ☐ 私はよく夜に家で動画を見ます。 | I often watch videos ____ home ____ the evening. |

### Unit 4　[週末にしたことを述べる／過去形]

| | |
|---|---|
| ☐ 私は日曜に花火大会に行きました。 | I _____ ____ the fireworks festival ____ Sunday. |
| ☐ 私たちは日本庭園を訪れました。それは美しかったです。 | We _____ a Japanese garden. It ____ beautiful. |

### Unit 5　[相手を励ます／可算名詞・不可算名詞]

| | |
|---|---|
| ☐ 次回はうまくいくように願っています。 | I hope _____ have better _____ next _____ ! |
| ☐ 私はホットドッグが食べたいです。コーヒーも1杯頼もうと思います。 | I want ____ hot dog. I'll order a _____ of coffee, too. |

## Unit 6 [これからすることを提案する／進行形]

| | |
|---|---|
| ☐ アンに電話してパーティーに招待しよう。 | Let's _____ Anne and _____ her to the party. |
| ☐ ベンは今、彼女に携帯メールを送っています。 | Ben ____ _____ his girlfriend now. |

## Unit 7 [助けを求める／WH疑問文]

| | |
|---|---|
| ☐ この箱を運ぶのを手伝っていただけますか。 | Is ____ possible for you to _____ me _____ this box? |
| ☐ あなたは（仕事として）何をしていますか。 | _____ do you ____ ? |

## Unit 8 [パーティーに誘う／動名詞・不定詞]

| | |
|---|---|
| ☐ 私たちの卒業パーティーに来ない？ | Do you _____ to come ____ our graduation _____ ? |
| ☐ 私は旅行代理店で働くことを決めました。 | I _____ ____ work at a travel agency. |

## Unit 9 [相手に約束する／未来形]

| | |
|---|---|
| ☐ どんなときもあなたを助けると約束します。 | I _____ I will always _____ _____ . |
| ☐ 私の友人は空港でインターンとして働くでしょう。 | My friend _____ _____ as an intern at the airport. |

## Unit 10 [好みを伝える／比較級・最上級]

| | |
|---|---|
| ☐ 私はパッケージツアーのほうが個人旅行よりもよいと思います。 | I _____ package tours _____ _____ than independent travel. |
| ☐ バスで旅をするほうが電車で旅をするよりも安いです。 | Traveling by bus is _____ _____ traveling by train. |

## 会話表現 & 基本例文一覧

### Unit 11　［同僚に確認する／助動詞］

| | |
|---|---|
| ☐ 私が先に、彼に名刺を渡すべきですか。 | _____ I _____ him my business card first? |
| ☐ あなたはお店の前に駐車することができます。 | You _____ _____ your car in front of the shop. |

### Unit 12　［喜びを伝える／現在完了形］

| | |
|---|---|
| ☐ あなたが入社してくれて嬉しいです。 | _____ _____ you joined our _____. |
| ☐ 私のボーイフレンドはカナダに行ってしまいました。3か月間会っていません。 | My boyfriend _____ _____ to Canada. I haven't _____ him for three months. |

### Unit 13　［滞在先の感想をたずねる／関係詞］

| | |
|---|---|
| ☐ そのレストランで食べた食べ物についてあなたはどう思いましたか。 | What did you _____ ___ the food that you _____ at the restaurant? |
| ☐ 紺色のスーツを着ている男性は私の上司です。 | The man _____ ___ wearing the navy suit is my boss. |

### Unit 14　［観光名所を案内する／受動態］

| | |
|---|---|
| ☐ パリは「愛の街」として知られています。 | Paris _____ _____ _____ the "City of Love." |
| ☐ 日本は毎年何百万人もの観光客に訪問されています。 | Japan ____ _____ by millions of tourists every year. |

### Unit 15　［お別れの言葉を述べる／接続詞］

| | |
|---|---|
| ☐ あなたの応援と励ましを私は決して忘れません。 | I'll _____ _____ _____ support and encouragement. |
| ☐ あなたが部屋を出る前に、電気を消してください。 | Please turn off the light _____ you _____ the room. |

## 不規則変化動詞一覧

| 原形 | 過去形 | 過去分詞形 |
|---|---|---|
| ☐ be「〜である」 | was / were | been |
| ☐ become「〜になる」 | became | become |
| ☐ bring「持っていく」 | brought | brought |
| ☐ buy「買う」 | bought | bought |
| ☐ catch「捕まえる」 | caught | caught |
| ☐ come「来る」 | came | come |
| ☐ do「する」 | did | done |
| ☐ drink「飲む」 | drank | drunk |
| ☐ draw「描く」 | drew | drawn |
| ☐ eat「食べる」 | ate | eaten |
| ☐ fall「落ちる」 | fell | fallen |
| ☐ find「見つける」 | found | found |
| ☐ forget「忘れる」 | forgot | forgot / forgotten |
| ☐ get「得る」 | got | got / gotten |
| ☐ give「与える」 | gave | given |
| ☐ go「行く」 | went | gone |
| ☐ have「持つ」 | had | had |
| ☐ hear「聞く」 | heard | heard |
| ☐ know「知る」 | knew | known |
| ☐ leave「去る」 | left | left |
| ☐ lose「失う」 | lost | lost |
| ☐ make「作る」 | made | made |
| ☐ meet「会う」 | met | met |
| ☐ pay「支払う」 | paid | paid |
| ☐ put「置く」 | put | put |
| ☐ read「読む」 | read | read |
| ☐ ring「鳴る」 | rang | rung |
| ☐ run「走る」 | ran | run |
| ☐ say「言う」 | said | said |
| ☐ see「見る」 | saw | seen |
| ☐ sell「売る」 | sold | sold |
| ☐ send「送る」 | sent | sent |
| ☐ sing「歌う」 | sang | sung |
| ☐ take「とる」 | took | taken |
| ☐ tell「話す」 | told | told |
| ☐ write「書く」 | wrote | written |

▶ ここからはがして下さい

このシールをはがすと
CheckLink 利用のための
「教科書固有番号」が
記載されています。
一度はがすと元に戻すことは
できませんのでご注意下さい。

4071 English Missions! Basic

CheckLink

---

本書にはCD（別売）があります

# English Missions! Basic

ミッション型 大学英語の総合演習：基礎編

2019 年 1 月 20 日　初版第 1 刷発行
2025 年 2 月 20 日　初版第10刷発行

著　者　Robert Hickling
　　　　臼　倉　美　里

発行者　福　岡　正　人
発行所　株式会社　金　星　堂
（〒101-0051）東京都千代田区神田神保町 3-21
Tel.　(03) 3263-3828（営業部）
　　　(03) 3263-3997（編集部）
Fax (03) 3263-0716
https://www.kinsei-do.co.jp

編集担当　蔦原美智　　　　　　　　　　Printed in Japan
印刷所・製本所／萩原印刷株式会社
本書の無断複製・複写は著作権法上での例外を除き禁じられています。
本書を代行業者等の第三者に依頼してスキャンやデジタル化すること
は、たとえ個人や家庭内での利用であっても認められておりません。
落丁・乱丁本はお取り替えいたします。

ISBN978-4-7647-4071-6　C1082